LESSONS *from* *the* MASTERS

Seven Keys to

Peak Performance

and Inner Peace

LESSONS *from the* MASTERS

Seven Keys to

Peak Performance

and Inner Peace

JIM BRAULT

Published in the United States by

Center Line Press
180 Somershire Dr. Suite 30
Rochester, NY 14617
[716] 342-1820
[800] 594-1249
To order additional copies of *Lessons from the Masters*, or to find out about our other products and services, call or write to us.

Editor: Jen Resnick
Project Coordinator: Akko Nishimura

Quotes from *Tao Te Ching* by Lao-tzu, a New English version, with foreword and notes by Stephen Mitchell, translation copyright 1988 by Stephen Mitchell. Reprinted by permission of HarperCollins Publishers, Inc.

First Edition

ISBN 0-9663482-0-6

Book Design and Cover Illustration: Yuko Uchikawa/Makers' Studio

To the memory of my mother - her example of love stays with me to this day.

To my father - I am only beginning to realize how much you have taught me.

To my wife, Jessie, and our children, Rachel, David and Daniel. Thank you all for being a constant reminder of the fun, happiness, chaos, spirit and love that life is.

I want to express my gratitude to the many individuals who have helped in the development of this book, either through their comments and suggestions as it took form, or by providing the guidance and teaching on which it is based.

To Jen Resnick, Akko Nishimura and Yuko Uchikawa, thank you for your patience, creativity and guidance in helping make this book what it is. To Kim Valentine, Leah Hanes, Dave Allman, Barry Farber, Christine Hutchinson, Peter Berg, Rich Cooper, Brian Biro, and my wife, Jessie, for their suggestions and guidance on the many manuscripts leading up to what you now hold in your hands.

Thanks to my training partners Don Bigelow, Jay Rowland, Jerry Tripani and William Faucette, Jr., and my Wing Chun students for their continued dedication and support.

I would like to thank my many teachers in the martial arts for their patience, guidance and commitment to helping others: Tae Kwon Do Masters Sang Chul Lee, Nam Yell An, Mark McCarthy, Sam J. Kim, Soon Ho Jeun, and Chung Sik Choi; Iado and Isshin Ryu Karate instructor Matt Dorsey; Tai Chi instructor John Solberg; Muay Thai Master Surachai Sirisute (Ajarn Chai).

I would also like to thank Mark Cannan for helping to open me to a whole new world: one in which seeing is through the heart.

My heartfelt appreciation, gratitude and respect goes out to Kevin Seaman, my teacher in Wing Chun, Jeet Kune Do, and occasionally Kali and Muay Thai. As much as you have taught me about the martial arts, you have taught me much more about life. You have no idea how many people you impact through your character, your compassion and your humility.

Finally, I would especially like to thank the masters who are highlighted in this book.

To Aaron "Jeff" McLeod: your leadership, your gentle strength, your patience, your conviction to do what is right, and your dedication to helping others serves as a shining example that there is a place for the spirit in the world of business.

To Gurucharan Singh Khalsa, my Kundalini Yoga and meditation teacher: you have shown me the power in gentleness, the strength in spirit. Thank you for sharing your wonderful "technology."

To Dan Inosanto: although I have had the privilege of spending only a short amount of time with you in person, you have taught me more than you'll ever realize. Your humility, dedication to the martial arts, and love for learning have helped me to grow, both in the martial arts and as a person.

To Francis Fong, my teacher in Wing Chun: your tireless enthusiasm for your art, your commitment to teaching and to elevating all those around you, and your sincere love of humanity make you without a doubt the most incredible person I have ever met.

CONTENTS

Do not seek to follow in the footsteps of the wise.
Seek what they sought.

—Zen Monk Basho

THE PATH OF MASTERY

You're in your house one day, maybe cleaning out a room or going through some old boxes, and you find a key. It's not one you recognize and you wonder what it opens. To satisfy your curiosity you go around the house trying it out on all your locks, but it ends up not matching any. So you throw it away, figuring you'll never need it.

Or maybe you don't. Maybe you keep the key just in case some day you run across the lock it was meant to open.

What if, years later, you were to discover a chest whose lock your key opens? When you open it, you are amazed to discover sparkling gems and wonderful treasures. Suddenly, something you had thought was worthless has new, unexplored value.

You really have the same potential in your hands here. *Lessons from the Masters* contains seven keys that can unlock a treasure chest full of valuable wisdom and priceless insights.

It is up to you whether or not you choose to use them. But I honestly believe that these keys can help you.

Here's why.

Our world is becoming faster paced by the minute. Over half of the Fortune 500 businesses that were on the list ten years ago are no longer there. Not just no longer on the list, but no longer in existence. One hundred and fifty years ago, the average work week was twenty eight hours. Then forty hours became the norm. A few years ago, people were predicting thirty hour work weeks due to "time saving" advances in technology. The reality is that the average person in the United States now works fifty three hours a week.

If I asked you if the world is more or less competitive than it was fifteen years ago, I'd be willing to bet that you would say more. If I asked you if it seems like you have to work harder just to break even, my guess is that you would say yes. Finally, if I asked you if you think that the world is going to slow down or speed up in the near future, you would probably just laugh.

As a nation, we are working harder and longer than ever before. We live in a hyper-competitive culture, one that is not about to slow down. And it's not just in the adult world. Years ago a teenager could walk on to the field or court as a high school freshman and have a chance to play a sport. Now, coaches only use the players who started at younger ages and already have developed skills. Kids who could learn but have no immediately apparent talent are left to languish on the bench. Today, we need to become peak performers just to be in the game.

But, you say, the upside is that all this extra effort is making us so much happier, right? I mean, we work harder, but we really are able to enjoy the fruits of our labor.

Yeah, right.

The average person today is a hundred times more likely to be depressed as they were a century ago, fifty times more likely than just thirty years ago. Prozac is the number one prescribed drug in America.

Little wonder. First we spend more time at work. Then, once we've accomplished our everyday chores—fix dinner, shop, make sure homework is done, teeth are brushed and lunches made—we have still to prepare our own children for their future with tutoring, dance, music, karate lessons, scouts and after school activities. Now can we relax? Not yet. To be a successful modern professional means we also have to be connoisseurs of the latest software, be able to navigate the internet, answer our e-mail, voice mail, phone messages and faxes, keep up with the world on CNN, and still have time to sculpt those all important buns of steel and rock hard abs. If we don't have the economic or social means to achieve these things, we are made to want them desperately by the media and culture of consumerism surrounding us.

There are many benefits to our culture, certainly. But it is also one that emphasizes results and material gain over almost anything else. "The bottom line" is the mantra for our age.

While at times we may be tempted with fantasies of going off to a remote island somewhere and blissing out, or climbing to the top of a mountain and forgetting this frenetic world, that isn't a realistic option for most of us. We have responsibilities: children, parents, friends, employees, and employers who count on us. And we have passions and projects, for work or creating something unique to ourselves, or simply watching our families grow and become strong.

What if it were possible, though, to have that level of external success: to perform at peak levels and have the inner peace that we all desperately need? What if it's not a trade-off? What if you could accomplish your worldly goals and at the same time experience mental, physical and spiritual harmony? What would that be worth?

It would be priceless, wouldn't it?

That is why I am so excited about sharing these Seven Keys with you. I honestly believe that using these keys will help transform your life from one of results to one of rewards, from one of short term wins to one of long term successes. Understanding these keys can help you produce the results you need, and the inner peace you seek.

For as long as I can remember I have been intrigued by masters. Although hard to describe, they are easy to recognize. Masters have achieved the highest levels in their disciplines, yet they possess something more.

There's a quiet knowing based on confidence built up by years of experience—a knowing that does not need to boast or brag. Humility which comes from the knowledge of where they started, and from the realization that everyone they meet has something of wisdom to offer. A calm approach to the world based on a lifetime of ups and downs, of triumphs and setbacks. Compassion for others based on an understanding that everyone has struggles and that we all have at sometime or other benefited by a kind word or a helpful suggestion. Passion for learning and sharing with others based on years of trial and error with partners and competitors also striving to be their best.

It is these qualities that enable mastery.

It is these qualities that separate a master from an expert.

We have all seen a lot of experts—individuals who possess a phenomenal talent, yet who destroy their health, their relationships, and their careers. Every day newspapers, magazines and TV programs explode with stories about exceptionally skilled athletes, business people and entertainers who have ruined their lives through drugs, violence and abuse. Though able to achieve their goals to excel in their chosen fields, they are unable to enjoy that very success they worked so hard to obtain.

But why? How can someone possess the tremendous discipline it takes to perfect their skills in one area, yet not have even a modicum of discipline when it comes to other aspects of their life? How could someone possess control over their body unimagined by most people, yet not be able to control their emotions? How could a person who has had the benefit of so many people helping them achieve their current level of success turn into a self-absorbed egomaniac who cares little for those who helped them get there?

Inner peace does not necessarily come with advanced skills, just like wisdom and happiness don't always come with old age. Mastery is more than just skill, more than physical abilities and mental facility. A master is able to combine discipline and control with an understanding of their own spirit and personal tendencies. A master approaches tasks, even more, their entire lives in a very different way that allows them to get excellent results while still enjoying inner peace. I call it *The Path of Mastery*.

The good news is that it can be learned.

I have the good fortune to have trained, worked and studied with some of the best teachers in the world, masters in their own right who have achieved the highest levels of success in their areas of expertise. They come from a variety of backgrounds, from martial arts, from yoga and meditation, and from Fortune 500 businesses.

Some of them are quite famous, while others are relatively unknown outside their respective circles; yet, they all are excellent examples of people who have chosen the path of mastery. Not only have they shared generously with me their knowledge of their own disciplines, but more importantly, they taught me what the path of mastery is and what it takes to live that way.

For, even though each of these teachers has spent their lives mastering very different disciplines, they all describe the path of mastery in the same way. So while some are masters of martial arts, others masters of yoga and meditation, and still others masters of international business, all of them agree on the principles of mastery.

That, for me, is a ringing signal of truth. If just one person described to me the path of mastery, it could simply be their style. But when another person detailed how they mastered their art and their life in the same way, then I got curious. When all of these masters gave me the same answers, I got excited. This told me that there were fundamental concepts or principles that could be learned. As one of my teachers repeated many times, "success leaves clues".

This agreement is important because the lessons from the masters are not simply my own conclusions. If they were, you might think, "that's nice, and I'm glad they seem to have worked for you, but..." And you would be justified in thinking that.

Yet they aren't just mine, nor are they simply one person's ideas with whom I have studied, nor are they a bunch of theories that don't cut it in the real world. Just the opposite. They have been tested in the sometimes harsh reality of the business world, in the violent and unforgiving ring of full contact competition, and in the quiet hours of contemplation when insight illuminates the entire soul.

These ideas represent the collective wisdom of many great teachers. Teachers who have tested and applied these concepts thousands of times over, concepts which also appear consistently in philosophy, manuals and scriptures of old. They are keys which have stood the test of time—as powerful and effective today as they were centuries ago—ancient methods still in use by wise teachers today.

To make these concepts accessible and easy to understand, I have distilled them into Seven Keys which lead to peak performance and inner peace. It is written as a collection of short stories, experiences and personal conversations with my teachers so that you can get a flavor of their wit and wisdom in addition to the lessons. I've also shared my own process of success and struggle to consistently apply these lessons.

The path of mastery is an approach to life. Notice that I don't call it the path *to* mastery, for that would connote a destination or an end-point. In an age of get-rich-quick schemes, total body fitness in just three minutes a day, and instantaneous gratification being promoted on the airwaves 24 hours a day, the path of mastery is not that sexy.

Sometimes it means taking the long road. Sometimes it means losing to ultimately win. As one of my teachers said to me: "Don't worry if it takes you a long time to learn this. The longer it takes you, the longer it will remain with you."

I wish I could say that I have applied these lessons my whole life. But as you'll discover in the pages that follow, I haven't. There have been periods in my life when I was more concerned with results than how I obtained them, more interested in what I could get instead of what I could give.

The nature of life is such that you'll get a result either way. I did, too. To me, the question isn't so much about the results you get in your life, as the kind of life that you get as a result.

Or, in the poetic words of Ursula K. LeGuin:

It is good to have an end to journey towards,
but it is the journey that matters, in the end.

My wish is that you benefit as much from these lessons as myself and others have. I trust that you will, because even though we all may lead very different lives in many respects, I also believe we're alike in a lot of ways and that we share many of the same struggles.

Let's begin.

Here are your keys.

The teacher opens the door, but you must enter by yourself.

—*Chinese Proverb*

THE FIRST KEY

BE YOUR BEST

This story doesn't end with the hero getting a black belt; for me that was only the beginning. The truth is, after a fleeting moment of exhilaration as I cinched it around my waist, I didn't feel any different than I had the day before. My white uniform was still the same: stained the color of my previous belt around the waist, worn out and lived in.

My feelings didn't change much with the second degree ranking, either. Yes, after ten years of sweating my guts out every day and going head to head in full contact competition, I had learned how to fight. But I thought there would be more. I felt that I should end up with something besides busted up hands and feet, two broken ribs and the inability to smile fully on my right side because of a caved-in cheekbone.

I thought I should feel better emotionally, be more in control. But the truth was that I wasn't any more patient or relaxed. If anything, I was more hyped up. Sometimes I was afraid of what I might do if I let my temper get the best of me, something that was happening more frequently.

So, before I tested for my third degree black belt I switched to another style of martial art. I figured it must have been the art's fault, not mine. After all, I had given it over a decade of full out devotion and it hadn't given me what I wanted.

The new style held my attention for a while, but after about two years, my interest once again waned. With a growing family and a demanding business to run, getting to practice was just another thing to cram into an already overcrowded schedule. The movements had become routine, a physical work out with no deeper meaning. Not so different from lifting weights.

Over the next few years I tried a couple more styles of martial arts, but they didn't give me what I was looking for any more than the first two did. I had to confront the fact that I had this fantasy notion that if I practiced martial arts, especially if I made it to black belt, then I would be like the blind Shaolin monk, Master Po, on the TV show *Kung Fu*—calm, peaceful, and at ease—whether dealing with an attacker or a mental challenge.

But I wasn't.

To be honest, getting a black belt wasn't the only thing that wasn't what I thought it was going to be. My life wasn't what I thought it would be, either. The funny thing is, I had everything I set out to get. I had excelled in high school and college wrestling, graduated with a Master's degree from an Ivy League school, was making a lot of money in my business, and I had a beautiful wife and three healthy, intelligent, well-behaved kids.

So what was the problem? I had everything I always wanted. Everything, apparently, but what I wanted most, because under the surface of my "successful" life, a sense of melancholy and disappointment pervaded my existence. It was a feeling that would not diminish no matter how many trophies I won, what belts I earned, or how much money I made. The pace of my world was getting more and more rapid, the responsibilities and demands on my time more rigorous. It was as if I was always on my way to something or somewhere else, certain that when I arrived there, then I would be happy.

The thing was, I kept arriving, to no avail. My happiness was fleeting at best. It would last for a little while, but ultimately it would fade and I would resume my search. It was as though I were driving from city to city to city in search of some thing to make me happy, though nothing ever did.

I didn't realize that no thing ever could.

When the student is ready,
the teacher will appear.

—Ancient saying

THE FIGHT WITHIN

It was an anomaly that I was even there. This was my first martial arts class of any kind in almost a year. I had been running and lifting weights to fill the void my martial arts practice had left.

Several weeks before, I had received a brochure in the mail for the Northeast Martial Arts Training Camp in Cortland, New York, about two and a half hours away from where I lived. It was a four day program and I couldn't take much time away from work. Still, it sounded pretty interesting. The camp featured four instructors. The first was Dan Inosanto, who was Bruce Lee's training partner and senior student. Then there was a guy named Larry Hartsell, who also had trained with Bruce Lee, and who specialized in grappling. There was a Muay Thai Master named Sirichai Sirisute, called "Ajarn Chai", and lastly a Wing Chun Kung Fu instructor named Francis Fong who, according to the brochure, "was considered by many to be one of the finest Wing Chun instructors in the country."

The only thing I knew about Wing Chun was that it was the art Bruce Lee had started with. I had a passing interest in Thai boxing, and thought it might be pretty cool to meet these guys that had trained with Bruce Lee, so for reasons not totally clear to me, I signed up for one day.

By the time we got to the lunch break I had already soaked completely through three T-shirts. The humidity of early June, combined with the four hours of training that we had already put in, left me exhausted. I was glad that I had only signed up for one day since we still had Wing Chun and Thai boxing to go.

About sixty students were assembled for the Wing Chun class. Some people talked casually with their friends, others stretched out as we waited for Francis Fong to arrive.

He arrived just before one o'clock. He bowed at the

entrance of the gym, then came around and shook everyone's hand with a smile and a warm hello. When he got to me I bowed and shook his hand with both of mine as a sign of respect. His grip was not overly firm, more like one you use with a friend that you see frequently. What felt like a current of electricity passed through my arm as he shook it. I hoped my face didn't register surprise at the sensation. Logically I chalked it up to dehydration and electrolyte imbalance, but deep down I knew that it was something more.

Though probably fifteen years older than me, his face was unlined, like that of a child's. He emitted a feeling of awesome power and supreme gentleness at the same time. He said hello in a way that made it feel as though we hadn't seen each other in a long time.

After Sifu Fong finished greeting everyone individually, Kevin Seaman, the director of the camp, introduced him as he had the other instructors. Sifu Kevin reminded us to address him as sir, or "Sifu," which is a title of respect in the Chinese martial arts. With a smile and a salute, Sifu Fong spoke.

"How many people here have ever studied Wing Chun before?"

A few hands raised.

"It's funny. People fight over which martial art is the best. The truth is that no one martial art is better than another. Different styles are good for different things. It all depends on the situation," he said in a rapid burst typical of a person from Hong Kong.

"The best defense is right here," he said pointing to his head, "or here," he joked, pulling the trigger on an imaginary gun. "That's all you need. You don't have to work out, just your one finger. You get a black belt right away. A bullet is faster than a punch any day," he said with what I would learn was a trademark grin.

"But in reality, martial arts are good for more than self-defense. They can help you understand yourself, then you can use that knowledge to help your life.

Don't separate your training from the rest of what you do. Use your practice to help you develop in other areas."

With that, Sifu Fong began teaching us his art.

Over years of practicing martial arts I have seen many magnificent displays of technical skill, amazing acrobatic routines, sheer power, and lightning-like moves. Yet, none of them compared to what captivated my attention over the next two and a half hours. Sifu Fong's explosive power and virtually incomprehensibly fast movements were simply astounding to watch.

But as quick as he was, he was even quicker to smile and offer an encouraging word.

My partner and I were having difficulty with many of the movements. We were trying to go quickly right away. He must have noticed because he came by.

"Don't try to rush through the moves. It's better to take the time and understand what you are training for. Some people get so stuck in rituals that they forget what they are doing it for. They just go through the motions. Don't let that happen to you," he said waving his finger back and forth.

"Use your martial arts practice to help you become a better person, that's the most important thing. After all, you may never get into a fight, but you're always fighting yourself. That's the only real fight."

Standing before me was perhaps the epitome of what I had been seeking in my practice for all those years, someone who seemed to have found a secret beyond the movements, someone who had mastered what to me had seemed to be the missing component: himself.

I wished then that I had signed up for all four days.

You may never get into a fight,
but you're always fighting yourself.

—Francis Fong

PRACTICE EVERYTHING, UNDERSTAND WHAT WORKS

I met Dan Inosanto back in 1990 at the Northeast Martial Arts Training Camp. I think most people, myself included, are initially attracted to him because he trained with Bruce Lee. In fact, he was his senior student and the man personally chosen by Bruce to carry on his Jeet Kune Do concepts.

As I got to know him a little better though, what impressed me more than his association with Bruce Lee, more than his thorough knowledge of an amazing number of martial arts, and more than his lightning-like speed, was his humility, his compassion and his understanding of human nature.

During one of his sessions at the camp, a student asked about different martial arts, wanting to know which was really the best form of self-defense. Since the Ultimate Fighting contests were just on the horizon, it was a timely question.

Guro Dan smiled. "You know, that's a question a lot of people have. Is Jujitsu better than Thai Boxing, or is Savate better than Karate? Can a Tae Kwon Do man beat a Kung Fu man?"

The student nodded his head.

"That's like asking is a grenade better than a hand gun," he said. "Is it?"

"It depends," the student answered.

"Exactly. It depends. In a phone booth a grenade's not the best weapon. But there are situations where a grenade is a superior weapon.

"Different arts are good for different things. You always have to look at the individual. People see someone winning with grappling techniques and they run out and study grappling. All these schools start offering grappling now.

"Then somebody wins with striking techniques, and people run out and study that."

That felt familiar. I thought of how corporations

also have management fads of the year. First TQM, Total Quality Management, is all the rage, then it's empowerment and teams, then Just-in-Time, and on and on. Each company promotes what's being heralded as the cure for management's ills, but in their eagerness to grab the solution, they may never analyze their own unique weaknesses and strengths. How often do we do that as individuals as we chase after the latest self-improvement fads, or exercise techniques, always looking outside of ourselves for the solutions?

"In the beginning of these contests a lot of the strikers didn't train in grappling techniques, so they got beat. Now you see the strikers working on their grappling, and they are doing much better. The same is true of the grapplers. They are developing their stand-up fighting skills." That made sense to me. Like rounding out your repertoire.

"But remember, it's not the style, it's the individual who does that style. It's what the person brings to the situation, their own talents. I remember when I started to get really interested in Filipino martial arts. Sifu Bruce encouraged me to study them, and one day I was practicing with the Kali sticks at the school."

Guro Dan bent down and picked up two 28 inch rattan sticks. "Bruce asked to see my sticks. He took them and showed me how he would fight with them. And in fighting in a way that made sense to him, given his knowledge of himself and martial strategies, he demonstrated a style that is used primarily on a certain island in the Philippines, never having even used Kali sticks before."

After a quick demonstration of the style, and an explanation of the origin and creators that I don't quite remember, he set the sticks back down.

"Bruce brought a certain level of proficiency to that style. Bruce was a phenomenal athlete. So if he used a certain style, then people say that it's the best. But there's no such thing. It depends on the person. Bruce used to say, 'Take what is useful and discard the rest.'

"That doesn't mean that you throw away a front kick after your first try because it didn't work."

Dan Inosanto acted out missing a kick and getting smacked in the face.

"You need to develop it to a certain level of proficiency. But after that, use what is useful for you based on your own attributes and talents. Use cross-training to help you develop your own personal style in the arts. Understand your own strengths to understand others. But, finally, use what allows you to grow as a martial artist and as a person."

> The goal of the martial arts
> is not for the destruction of an opponent,
> but rather for self growth and self perfection.
>
> —*Dan Inosanto*

I didn't see Sifu Fong again for another six months. Kevin Seaman usually brings him up to central New York only twice a year: four days in early June for the camp, and two days in late fall by himself.

This time, I sent in my registration fee as soon as I received the flyer in the mail announcing the November program. I had been diligently practicing the Wing Chun Kung Fu I had learned from the summer camp, and was anxious to learn more. With each passing day I grew more excited about training with Sifu Fong once again, and doubled the intensity level of my workouts in anticipation of the session.

The weekend finally arrived, and I was ready. As we warmed up and prepared for the start of the class I looked around at the other participants, unconsciously comparing myself with them. I bet that no one else had been training as hard as I had. I was looking forward to demonstrating what I had learned in the last six months.

Sifu Fong had us begin with a drill we had learned in the summer camp. With a self-satisfied smile, I launched into the movements with great gusto. This was one I had been practicing religiously for months. I was confident that my hard work would reveal itself in my flawless technique. I kept looking for Sifu Fong out of the corner of my eye to notice how well I was doing.

Finally he came around to my partner and me.

He shook his head. "Take it easy. You're trying too hard," he said. He adjusted every part of me: the position of my feet, my hips, my arms, my head, where I was looking. He instructed me to try it again.

Though this was not quite the feedback I had expected, once more I attempted the movement, convinced I had it down pat. Once again he shook his head. I could feel the tension in my back as I became more and more frustrated over my inability to get this move down. After all, I had been practicing it for almost half a year, and besides, I held a second degree black belt, had been training in martial arts for over ten years, and had seven years of wrestling to boot. I thought, "How hard could this be?"

It was a lot harder than I thought. I couldn't seem to get any of the movements right. Clearly I was missing something.

"Relax, take your time," Sifu Fong said at least a half dozen times that first day alone. Try as I might, I just couldn't seem to do any of the techniques very well, even the ones I thought I had mastered. I was dejected after the day's session.

As we were wrapping up, Sifu Kevin invited the students to join him, his wife Charlene and Sifu Fong for dinner. Traditionally, instructors don't mingle with the students, so I jumped at the chance. I found my foul mood lightening as I drove over to the restaurant.

We went to a small Chinese place near the school. The decor left something to be desired, but the food was delicious. Somewhere during the second course one of the students brought up a question about the term Grand Master.

Sifu Fong laughed. "You know, I never heard this term Grand Master until I came here from Hong Kong in 1973. It's all marketing. I understand why the instructors do it. People want to be better than some-one else. So if somebody else is a master, then they have to be a Grand Master. Understand? They always try to one-up somebody else. They compare. If they have a better title then they feel superior."

I felt my face flush. I had gone into the session that morning thinking myself superior to the others there, when in fact it was just a cover-up for my feelings of insecurity over my limited abilities in that style. Though I may have had genuine skill in other martial arts, Wing Chun was still very new for me, and the truth was that I was a brand new beginner, not very skilled at all.

"Don't try to be better than somebody else. Don't try to be the best. Whenever you do that, then you have to compare yourself to other people. You either think you are better, or not as good. Who cares? Everyone should try to help each other get better. Instead, concentrate on being *your* best."

For me, that lesson was the most important of the entire weekend. Actually, one of the most important lessons I had learned in many years.

"People try to master all these different arts. They think they can master ten different styles."

He shook his head and smiled. "No way, it's impossible. Maybe one, if they are lucky. If you want to be a master of anything—a martial art, playing an instrument, business—it takes a long time and a lot of practice. Years and years. There are no short cuts, believe me," he said.

"But being a master of yourself is more important. What does it matter how many people you can knock out if you're not happy with yourself? Nobody cares. If you aren't happy with yourself you'll never make anyone else happy either. You'll always be looking to get other people to make you feel a certain way. Makes sense? Like if they are a master, then you have to be a Grand Master to feel good."

I nodded my head.

"Some people think if they acquire some advanced skills then they will become a master and they won't have any problems. Or they think that if they go sit next to a Grand Master then they'll get his energy."

He leaned back, closed his eyes, and spread his arms out wide. "Oh, his energy is very strong. I got it!"

We all laughed, but mine was a nervous laugh as if to say, "Hah, how idiotic. How could anyone think that?" when deep inside I knew that I had come to that seminar with a desire to be a Wing Chun master. I wanted to be able to move gracefully like him, possess a cat-like command over my body like he did his. I wanted the easy confidence I saw in him and thought if I could just master the physical techniques, the rest would come free. I had been looking for mastery on the outside, instead of addressing it from the inside, the only place it ever comes from anyway.

"In reality, nothing could be further from the truth. Mastery is something you uncover, it's within you already. But here, we are led to believe that we're not good enough. Only if you buy this product, then you'll be perfect."

"Until the next product comes along," Sifu Kevin said.

"That's right. So many people think that all their problems will be solved if they just get a black belt or if they become a master. You know? It's crazy. I don't even like the term master. Sifu is better. *Si* means teacher, *fu* means father. So it's a teacher who loves you like a father, watches out for you. Sensei is the same thing in Japanese."

It was very apparent that Sifu Fong did care for his students beyond their level of proficiency in martial arts.

"Technique means nothing. It does in the sense of martial arts, but in life…" He shook his head, preferring to let his body finish the sentence. "Your character is more important, what you have in your heart."

Sifu Fong took a drink of tea and was silent for a moment before he continued.

"Mastery isn't something you get, especially from somebody else. You already possess it inside. You would understand this if you just let go of the things that hold you back from realizing it. Believe in yourself, be true to yourself. If you are happy inside and are honest with yourself, loyal to your own values, then everything will work out."

Another sip. "Keep working on mastering something. You have to do that for your business or career. And if you like martial arts then keep on working to master that, too. It's good for you, helps keep you healthy. But remember, all of that work is for nothing if you don't master yourself. That's really the only thing worth mastering," he said.

After a long pause he added, "And by far the hardest."

Knowing others is intelligence;
knowing yourself is true wisdom.
Mastering others is strength;
mastering yourself is true power.

—*Lao-tzu, Tao te ching*

THE CINNAMON SISTERS

The azure water of St. John's Maho Bay sparkled as the early morning rays lit up the sky. With the sound of tropical birds lilting over the water, the island woke from its slumber. We had just completed a yoga kriya, a set of exercises, breathing and meditation, led by Gurucharan Singh Khalsa. Until a few months before, I had never met a yogi.

Prior to meeting Gurucharan, I had owned a personal development and sales training franchise of Anthony Robbins. While it was very fulfilling in some respects, after four years I longed to do something more. I wanted to expand my offerings to my students. One of those students, a guy named Mark Cannan, taught yoga, and asked if I would consider setting up a yoga and meditation workshop at my training center. I said that I would, and after a few calls we had over thirty people signed up for a two hour introductory course.

I found the exercises intriguing, and continued on with the eight week class that followed. Mark informed me that he was bringing his teacher to Rochester for a weekend event, and asked if I wanted to go. As it turned out, by then I was just about completing the sale of my training franchise, and was in the process of starting a sales and marketing consulting firm. By the end of the weekend I had Gurucharan as my first client.

But he became more than my client. He also became my teacher and friend. As I helped him learn about marketing and sales, he helped me learn about meditation, yoga, and finding an inner peace that was missing in my life.

One of the ways we reached other people was to sponsor retreats to exquisite locations such as Maho Bay, where we would practice yoga, meditate, and learn more about how to manage our internal environments in order to better deal with our external ones. A group of twenty had come to Maho Bay for a week long session on temperament.

Gurucharan Singh Khalsa sat peacefully on his sheepskin rug, his massive frame covering the majority of it. He silently surveyed his surroundings, then began his talk on temperament.

"You know, it's really pretty funny. Everyone can accept that vegetables are different. They look different, taste different, ripen at different times of the season. Right? And we can all accept that animals are different. Like dogs. Little dogs, what are they called? The ones that yip, yip, yip all the time and shake."

"Yorkshire Terriers," someone replied.

"No, the real little...Chihuahuas! That's it." Gurucharan smiled.

"When you go to buy a dog, you know that they have different strengths and problems based on the breed. German Shepherds are great watch dogs, but they need to run a lot and get hip problems. Saint Bernards have heart problems and drool a lot, like some old people. But they are excellent as rescue dogs. But when it comes to us, we have difficulty believing that kind of thing. In the United States everyone thinks that you can be whoever and whatever you want. Think about it. If you want to become a U.S. citizen, what do you have to do? Memorize the states, know who your senator is, recite the Pledge of Allegiance, and take an oath. That's it. Then you're an American."

He shook his head. "Try that in India, or China, or Japan. You can work there, you can speak the language, and you can live there for years and years, but no matter how long you do, you won't be Indian, or Chinese or Japanese. You will never be accepted that way. So the U.S. is different. We are more accepting of other cultures, the melting pot and all that. But in some ways it is bad because people don't always accept themselves in the way that makes them unique. They're always trying to be someone else. They move to a different part of the country, get a new job, a new hairstyle, a new identity. They even change their name. You can do that here. So these people erase their past and start totally fresh. What's the problem with that?" Gurucharan asked.

Finally, after what seemed like five minutes someone said, "Sometimes people jump around changing who they think they are and they never get a good sense of themselves."

"Which means what?"

"People try to be something they're not."

"Hmmm. Interesting. Don't get me wrong. We can change a lot of things. We can influence our own characteristics, personal power and all that. At the same time, there must be a realization that there are certain tendencies that you will always have."

Gurucharan looked us all over with a sparkling eye. "So if you're a tomato, then you're a tomato. A brussel sprout, then a brussel sprout. And the tomato should grow to be as ripe, full and juicy as it can. And the brussel sprout should grow as hard, and small and awful-tasting as it should," he laughed.

"Just kidding. My apologies to all of you brussel sprout fans. The problem occurs when the tomato wants to be a brussel sprout, and vice versa. You get vegetable envy. There is a lack of respect and appreciation for what and who you are. If you get caught up in comparisons and jealousy you'll never become who you can be. You'll never fulfill your potential. You'll be spending your time worrying about how you're not good enough."

After a pause, he continued, "Understand what your strengths and weaknesses are. Do that through your practice. They will become clear. Do that through your meditation. You will see yourself for who you truly are. Be happy with your strengths. Also understand the areas that need more focus and development and be happy with that, too. But don't try to be somebody else. It will never work. Just be yourself."

"What kinds of things do you mean, Gurucharan?" one of the students asked.

"Let me share some research with you," he replied. "There have been a lot of studies done with monozygotic twins. You know, identical twins that were separated at birth and raised by two different families in different parts of the country."

I didn't think that sort of thing happened enough to make a reliable study, but apparently it did.

"One set of twins were found when they were forty two years old. Both had the same hairstyle, and both had the same type of job. That you might be able to explain," he said. He nodded his head.

"But then the study went on to say that they both owned the same breed of dog, and the dogs had the same name. And not a typical name, either. It was a weird name. And I remember reading this and thinking, 'is there a gene for naming dogs?'

"So listen, it gets better. Both of them had their socks in the second drawer of their bureaus, and they both had the same brand, arranged by color, lined up in the same order!

"Finally," he continued, "they were both neat freaks. Interestingly, the difference was in the way each of the twins explained their behavior. When asked about being neat, one of them said, 'Well of course I am. My mother was such a slob I had to be.' The other twin said, 'My mother was so anal about things being clean, I guess I just picked it up from her.'"

Gurucharan smiled.

"See, we make up stories about why we are a certain way. We rationalize our inborn characteristics."

Before I could really consider all the ramifications of the research he drove his point home by telling us about another study done on a pair of twins whom researchers found when they were eight years old and dubbed the 'cinnamon sisters.'

Gurucharan resumed his story. "The researchers had interviewed the mothers about a whole host of topics, one of which was the girls' eating habits. One of the mothers replied, 'Oh, she's such a fussy eater. Always picking. She's such a pain. I can hardly get her to eat anything at all. The only way I can do it is if I put cinnamon on it. Then she'll eat anything.' Now, interestingly enough, when they asked the other mother about her daughter, she had a totally different response. 'She's an angel. She's always been a good eater. Put cinnamon on it and she'll eat anything.'"

We all chuckled at this example of two different explanations of the same situation.

"So, as you go through your life, realize that there will be things that you excel at, and things that are more difficult for you. Part of that is just how you are wired. Try your best, certainly. But understand that your result will not be the same as someone else's. Just like the St. Bernard will never be a German Shepherd. Don't compare. Help each other; appreciate your differences."

And, I thought, try not to be like the mothers of the cinnamon sisters, placing so much judgment on those differences.

"You be the best you can be. That's all you can be. And that is enough."

In the landscape of spring,
the branches grow naturally.
Some long, some short.

—*Zen saying*

THE SECOND KEY

TAME YOUR
MONKEY MIND

When the mind cannot relax, all efforts fail.

—*Yogi Bhajan*

There is a story about a young boy who dreamed of being the greatest swordsman ever. He traveled far from his village and presented himself to the best teacher Japan had to offer.

"I wish to be the greatest swordsman that ever lived," he told the teacher. "How long will it take me to master the sword?"

The teacher waited a moment before responding. "If you practice diligently, I should think about ten years."

The boy shook his head. "That's too long. I don't have that much time. What if I practice all day, every day? Then how long?" he asked.

"In that case, twenty years," came the reply.

"Twenty years?" the boy exclaimed. "What if I did nothing else, just practiced the sword, all day and all night, and swore off all other activity?"

"In that case, forty years," the master answered.

Confused, the boy asked, "How come the harder I work, the longer it takes?"

And the master answered, "With your mind always fixed on the outcome, it will never relax. And if your mind cannot relax, you will never achieve mastery."

The lesson taught by this simple story is extremely difficult to learn. That is due, in part, to the paradox it presents to our society. Most of us in the West are taught that if you want to succeed, you have to persevere, set goals, take action, and follow through. Aphorisms like *No pain, no gain*, and *Put your nose to the grindstone* are taught to us as children and accurately reflect the belief system that most people in an industrialized culture hold as necessary to succeed in any endeavor.

But if we examine the teaching methods of the masters of old, we see an entirely different approach. An approach based on nature, and in keeping with the cycles and rhythm found in an agricultural society.

In a factory, there is always the sense that processes can be sped up, that cycle times can be reduced, and that if you work harder then the result will be better. And often, strictly in terms of production, those assumptions are accurate.

On a farm, however, those ideas don't apply quite as well. You can't rush the growth process. You can't force things to be ripe just because it's the end of the fiscal quarter. That's not to say that improvements can't be made, but results also have their own schedule, one that cannot always be rushed with increased effort. There is a time for planting, a time for nourishing, a time for harvesting, and a time for waiting.

The waiting is aided by the knowledge that if allowed to ripen at its natural pace, the fruit will be all the sweeter. The same concepts were historically utilized by martial arts teachers who taught their arts not for immediate application in tournament competition, but rather to prepare their students for life and death battles. Years ago, martial arts teachers would not let their students practice any technique for at least three years. Students swept the floors, cooked meals and carried the firewood. They were not permitted to practice with the others or even speak of martial arts.

At first this approach may be very difficult to understand. Why would you want to waste time doing menial labor when you could be practicing and improving your skills?

But, within a concept of cycles of growth, and patience for the time growth takes to happen, the teachers understood that they first had to prepare the foundation upon which to build and develop skills. Without a strong and healthy physical body, and a mind unencumbered by desires and anxiety, it was believed that any other skill development would be weak. So first teach the mind to relax. Prepare the soil. Once accomplished, then skills could be taught, just as properly cultivated soil will provide the seeds with a better chance of taking root and flourishing.

For us, as Westerners, this apparent clash of approaches provides an interesting dilemma. Do we set goals, review them daily, and tenaciously and persistently cling to what we desire? There are many people who will tell you that is how they have succeeded in life.

Or do we relax, and let events take their course, not focusing so much only on the outcomes? Certainly there are many cases in which people have succeeded under those circumstances.

Nowadays, even though we may want to take the time to relax our minds, such an approach seems impossible given the competitive situations in which we may find ourselves. Most of us don't feel we have the time; we want to get up to speed right away in order to hit the ground running. In the bottom line, results-driven mentality that is symptomatic of much of our society, we are expected to reap a harvest right away, every quarter.

As you'll discover in this lesson, we do need to keep our sights on our outcomes—that is, remain true to our intentions. But we also need to be flexible in the approach. It is a balance between staying the course, and allowing yourself to deviate from the path when it makes sense. It is being able to know when to persevere and hold on, and when to let go and try a different approach.

It is not, then, a choice between one approach and another. Instead, it is blending the elements of both methods to achieve an ultimate outcome that is better than either single approach.

This second key was probably the biggest lesson for me. Because in order to learn it, I had much to unlearn first. For years I had done very well following the *No pain, no gain* mentality. I formulated a plan,

37

established specific goals, then worked extremely hard in order to achieve those goals. I did that in everything: school, athletics, and later in business. If I had trouble with something, I would put my head down and go harder. I would shut out anything and anyone else and focus on what I had to do, and by God I did it, through hard work, perseverance and discipline. Only, in the long run, the results left me feeling alone and unfulfilled.

For me, the "monkey mind" is a great analogy, one that has changed my concept of effort and reward, and of working with others rather than going it alone. It is the first story in the second key, and one that accurately serves as a theme for the rest of the stories contained therein.

THE MONKEY MIND

"Do you know one way people catch monkeys?" Gurucharan asked me.

"No, sir, I don't."

"Monkeys are terrific thieves. They get into everything, and they are very fast. But they are also very stubborn, and that is their downfall. So the monkey catchers put fruit into a long neck bottle which is secured, and they make it so the monkey can just reach in to get the fruit," he said as he stretched out his arm. "Then he wraps his greedy little paw around it and is trapped."

"How?" I said.

"Because he won't let go. He is so stubborn that he holds on to the fruit, even when the men are coming to get him. And his fist with the fruit is too big to get through the opening of the bottle. He is so intent on holding on to his prize that he never lets go and gets in trouble."

"I never heard that before. That's pretty interesting," I said.

"And kind of dumb, too, isn't it?" he said stroking his beard.

"Yes, it is."

"Except that we do the same thing. We're just as dumb. The only difference is that we cling to pride, to looking good, to money, to sex, to being liked, to status, to winning, and much, much more. See, the monkey will only hold on to the fruit. We hold on to lots more."

"That's true," I said.

"So when you sense you are clinging to something, let it go."

"Anything?"

"Yes, anything. Just notice it. Someone pays you a compliment, 'Oh, you are such a great person!' Smile and say 'thank you,' and let it go. Someone else criticizes you, smile and say 'thank you,' and let it go. It's all the same, anyway. It's all an illusion."

I weighed what he said for a moment. "Okay, I get what you are saying there, I think. Wouldn't someone who was that detached be kind of a jerk, though?"

He smiled. "I didn't say detached. That is different. That's not caring, that's inhumane, a sociopath. Be non-attached."

"I'm not quite sure I'm following you."

"Think of it this way. You go to a movie. If you were attached to the movie, you would never leave. You would believe that the characters were real, not some imaginary characters on a screen.

"Now if you were detached, you might go to the movie and act like you weren't even there. You wouldn't look at the screen, you wouldn't pay attention. Your friends ask if you want some popcorn, but you don't answer. They say, 'What's wrong? Why are you in such a bad mood?' Then they don't invite you back anymore. You have no friends.

"Being non-attached is what you should strive for. You go, enjoy the movie, you get scared, or laugh, or cry, you experience and feel everything. You may remember it, but you regard it as a movie, as it should be. That the characters are not real, and they will probably be back in something else. The sequel. But that's it."

I nodded my head. "Yes, sir. I understand it in that context. But what about with a business, or something really important like your family? How can you be non-attached to that?"

"Pay attention. Pay attention to your family, and your business. But don't let your ego get caught up in it. The non-attachment is to your ego, to what's in it for you, not to your attention or your personal interest. See, in a business, your ego will worry, 'What if I lose money? What if I don't know the answer? What if I lose my business? How good am I doing?' All the ego.

Instead of the conscious mind working at how to make it a more profitable and better company."

"So pay attention to it, but don't care? What about goal setting, and focus, and…"

Gurucharan raised his hand to cut off my questions. "With your wife, do you always treat her the way she needs, or does it have to do with what you expect in return?"

I was beginning to answer when he cut me off again.

"Don't worry, I know the answer," he laughed.

I laughed too, because he was right. I guess I wasn't totally selfless; I was generally looking to get something.

"Most times love is selfish. Why does the same love that can be so beautiful also have the potential to bring about the most pain, jealousy and hatred? Because it was not a pure, selfless love with no expectation in return. It was a give to get love, a selfish love. If I do this for you, then I expect that.

"When your children were infants, you loved them totally and purely. They didn't smile yet, they didn't thank you. All they did was cry, dirty their diaper, sleep or sit there. But didn't you love them?"

"Yes, of course."

"Why?"

"Because…I just did," I said.

"With no expectation in return, right?"

"No, sir."

"But how do you feel when you hold a baby? Fantastic, because you are feeling pure love, not selfish love. When they get older, then you withhold your love based on whether they cleaned their room or not, or did well in school, or play nicely with each other."

I wondered how true that was for me. I knew I loved my children totally, even unconditionally, but I knew I didn't always show that love unconditionally. We talked some more about the monkey mind.

"It's the ego attachment to watch out for. Love in its pure form has no ego associated."

"So it's the monkey love I better watch out for, huh, sir?"

Gurucharan laughed. "Hah, that's a good one. You need to tame the monkey mind through constant practice. That is the first great lesson for you to master."

"Okay, but how do I do that?" I said.

Gurucharan patted me on the shoulder. "Another time," he answered and walked off.

I felt like I was on the receiving end of the old joke, "How do you keep an idiot in suspense? I'll tell you tomorrow."

I wish I had learned this lesson of the monkey mind a few years earlier.

After graduate school I went to work as a Human Resource representative for a company in Boston. Like all new hires, I didn't get vacation for my first six months. It was summertime, and Jessie wanted to take Rachel to visit her parents, so off they went while I stayed in Boston and worked.

Back then Jessie used to cut my hair. It was getting a bit too long for my taste, and I should have asked her to cut it before she left, but I didn't, so after a couple of days I felt really uncomfortable about the length of my hair. I got fixated on the idea that my hair was too long, and I wouldn't let it go (yes, I can see my hand in the bottle right now).

Not wanting to wait the two days until she got home, I got the brilliant idea to trim it myself. I know better than to try with scissors, so I elected to use a "hair thinner." It's a kind of automatic comb which is supposed to control how much hair is cut at once. I'm in the shower washing away when I get the brainchild of an idea that I'll just trim my hair. I get the thinner, and make three swift, what I thought were light, strokes under the shower head and with my eyes closed.

I open them to see three huge clumps of dark brown hair by my feet. Holding my breath, I reach up to assess the damage. I feel stubble. I had selectively given myself a brush cut in three places on the top of my scalp. I just about had a cow. What was I going to do?

Fortunately it was a Friday night, and I didn't have to go to work the next day. When I showed up at Logan International on Sunday to pick them up, Jessie immediately asked about the hat that I was wearing since I never wear hats.

"Nothing."

"What did you do?" she said in the exact same voice you would use with your dog when you brought him to the pile of crap he just dumped in the middle of your living room rug.

Slowly and painfully I removed my cap to reveal three white blotches. This was the middle of summer, and I had a decent tan, and kind of long hair. So the white scalp stood out really, really well against my almost black hair and tan face.

Having only been on the job for three weeks, I couldn't get a brush cut—a little too out there. Instead, every morning, I would brush my scalp with Jessie's mascara to hide the patches, then put a ton of gel in my hair so that when I combed it over the spots it would stay. Kind of like bald guys attempt to do, and I'm sure it looked about as good.

For three weeks I went to work with totally greased-back hair. My co-workers would comment: "Oh?! You got a new look," probably thinking the whole time, "Who is this freak we hired?" Being five foot five, I didn't want anyone to get too close to me and see the bald spots and mascara, so I would always back up when someone significantly taller got within three feet of me.

We sure do crazy things when we get our minds set on something. A poor haircut and a month of

43

humiliation is nothing compared to some of the bottles we allow ourselves to get stuck in.

I left that job after twenty months, and, no, it wasn't anything to do with the haircut. I wanted to have more of an impact with people than that job would allow me, so I began a search for a business to buy. People thought I was nuts. Here I had gone to graduate school for two years, then I switched fields after less than the two years it took me to go to school to get the job. In fact, I had no idea what I was going to do. I only knew the direction that I wanted to head in, and knew that my present course was not getting me there.

Many of them said, "You'll never get another job in a company again." At the time, I didn't care, because I didn't think I would ever work for a company other than one I owned. In the eight years that followed I had three businesses, each one sold to go in a somewhat different direction. When, at the end of that time, I applied to Fortune 500 companies for a position, again people told me that no company would hire me because I didn't have continued experience in one area.

But as it turned out, my willingness to let go of businesses and jobs that no longer supported my intentions turned out to be what got me hired. My new employers liked my diverse background and thought that it would allow me to bring a different perspective to the company. And, I hope, they could see that my path, for all its shifts, had some integrity to it. Had I listened to those around me and clung to a job which was not taking me where I wanted to go, I could never have set out on my own path of self discovery. It was scary to let go of that secure position and jump off into the unknown, and I didn't always land on my feet, but by being flexible and allowing my choices to reflect what I truly desired, not just what would keep me safe, I wound up with a much more suitable position.

The monkey mind is a lot like the ego. It likes to hold on to what looks bright and shiny, and its single minded tenacity often results in our getting caught in uncomfortable or even dangerous situations. In achieving our goals, we need to be able to step back and not confuse the ego's need for immediate gratification with what is consistent with our longer term direction. That is not to say to quit when the going gets tough, or to change with every little shift in the winds. Instead, it is a lesson to remind us that the ego will get attached to things that are not always in our best interest in the long run. That we need to learn how to detach ourselves from the ego's desire, so that we can align ourselves with higher principles.

In the beginner's mind there
are many possibilities.
But in the expert's mind, there are few.

—Shunryu Suzuki

A MIST IN THE PULPIT

I had a feeling that I would like him the moment we met. He has a way about him that immediately puts people at ease. Aaron "Jeff" McLeod was born and raised in a small town in Alabama called Dothan. Many southern colloquialisms spring forth when he speaks. Also evident is his country hospitality.

If you have ever dealt with most senior level managers in Fortune 500 businesses, you know that you have about thirty seconds to get to the point or they will do it for you. With Jeff, however, you get the sense of sitting on his front porch sipping lemonade when talking with him. He has a patient, soothing quality about him that makes you feel like you are the only person in the world just then, and that nothing else is more important than the conversation between the two of you. It's a quality that engenders a sense of loyalty that is almost unheard of in this day and age.

"Jeff, I know some of the pressures you must face. With what's going on in the market, and the relentless focus on earnings, you must have to deal with more than I could even begin to imagine. Yet, I don't think that anyone could ever tell. At least not here. You never seemed rushed or stressed, ever!" I remarked during one of our private development sessions. He held them with each of his directly reporting managers. "How do you do that?"

Jeff gave me one of his famous ear to ear dimpled grins. He looked down and laughed as if he'd been caught at something. I have worked with many good managers over the years, men and women in charge of multi-million and multi-billion dollar businesses. Of those people, only a few would I consider leaders. Of those, Jeff was by far the best.

"Well, there's a saying I like that says, 'If there's a mist in the pulpit there'll be a fog in the pew.'"

I laughed because I had heard him use it on more

than one occasion.

"So if I get panicked, then those around me will pick that up. And if people are panicked they usually won't make the best decisions."

"I see."

"Rarely, rarely, is there a need to act right away. Unless there's a fire or some emergency, most situations benefit from thinking things through a bit. Talking them out."

"So what allows you to do that? I mean, what do you believe that allows you to have that patience?" I asked. I told him that in the past, when I owned my own businesses, my tendency when I felt a lot of pressure was not to communicate. Rather I would shut down, and put my nose to the grindstone.

"Yeah, that's a pretty common reaction. What I have found, though, is that most times the answer lies within the problem."

"The answer lies within the problem?" I repeated.

"Right. If you give people the opportunity, they will almost always figure it out for themselves. So it's important to let them talk about, debate, even argue about a topic. As long as they maintain respect for each other, I'll let it go. Then in that way, they develop the ability to handle that situation and others that come along, too. Now if they get off into the weeds, then I'll bring it back around, but people need to experience and think things through on their own."

I thought about how many opportunities I had let slip by because of my need to get an immediate answer instead of relaxing and letting things take their course.

"Money will come, and money will go. You have to do your best to manage the business, the same time realize that there will be ups and downs. The opportunity lies in helping your people develop so that you can deal with the good times and the bad. And you can't do that effectively if you panic," Jeff said.

The conversation shifted to other topics, and soon

the hour and a half was up. As I rose to leave, Jeff added one parting thought.

"There's a saying that my father must have said a thousand times. I can picture it as clear as day. It was kind of a spin from something in the Bible. He said, 'If you faint in the day of adversity, your strength is small.' Your strength is small," he repeated.

Later that evening, I had the opportunity to immediately put into practice what Jeff had taught me. David and Danny, my sons who are two years and two days apart, were arguing over something important like who was sitting where. Though I knew all about reflective listening and conflict resolution, my general tendency at home had often been to yell. Even though I knew it didn't solve the problem, and it certainly didn't help them develop skills to deal with the situation, it did get them to be quiet.

But after what Jeff had said, I knew that wasn't the right approach. The phrase "your strength is small" kept ringing in my ears as I took a deep breath and headed into the living room. I spent a few quiet minutes with the boys, and, using one of my conflict resolution techniques, I asked each one to restate to the other's satisfaction what his brother's viewpoint was. Within five minutes, once they had clarified what each other's points were, they had settled their differences. And I didn't even have to yell.

Since that time, I can say with all honesty that I have changed my approach to my children. I saw the effect Jeff had on me and others. We *wanted* to do a good job for him. And because he allowed us the freedom to do the job the way we thought best, we often came up with better solutions. With my kids, my approach now is to expect less and encourage more. When I do that, I always get more than I ever expected.

If you faint in the day of adversity,
your strength is small.

—*Proverbs 24:10*

THE BEST PRESENT

"If your family could change one thing about you, what would it be?" The Zen master asked me that question after we had just been meditating in complete silence.

There were twenty-two of us attending a training workshop to become distributors for Anthony Robbins.

It was difficult to say the least. We each had to stand up in front of the group and answer one question. We might as well have been naked because the master had a way of seeing right through us. Some participants broke down and cried as his insightful questions went to the core of their pain.

Although I did not break down, he nevertheless struck a nerve with the question he has posed to me.

"To be there when I'm there," I finally managed.

"Meaning?" he probed.

"Meaning that when I'm in their presence I am not always present. I'm usually thinking about something else. What happened in the past, or what will happen. A lot about business. I tend not to live in the present moment to the extent that I would like."

One evening, a few months later, I was reviewing some material for a training program I was to give the next day. As I read, I was munching on a bowl of popcorn. Before I knew it, I was down to only kernels. I thought, somewhat whimsically: "If only I had known, I would have savored the last bite."

My thoughts flashed back to the master's question.

If I wasn't careful, I thought to myself, my life would end up like this popcorn bowl, with me not paying attention until it was over. "Hey, if I had known, I would have savored it."

OK, so big deal, so I didn't savor the last bite of popcorn. But if I didn't focus on the little things, what made me think I would do so with the important things? That's like someone messing up in practice but telling their coach, "Don't worry, when it comes to game time I'll do it right."

Sure you will.

In martial arts we have plenty of opportunity to be present. If we aren't, we get immediate feedback from our partners or our own bodies.

In everyday life, we do too. For instance, when you eat, don't take another bite of food until you have completely enjoyed the first. Take your time, savor the aroma, the look, the taste. Don't simply rush to the next bite without enjoying the one you're on.

In conversation, focus on the person. Pay attention to what they are saying, the words, their tone of voice and body language. Just listen. Don't think about what you will say next or how clever you can sound—just relax and be present.

I especially make sure I am present with my children. Everyone keeps telling me that they'll grow up so quickly. I want to make sure that I enjoy them now.

So when you find your mind drifting to something other than what you are doing in the moment, take a second to ground yourself. You can balance yourself by bringing your palms together, closing your eyes and taking a few deep breaths. It's no coincidence that this restful pose is a universal position of prayer and meditation the world over.

Practice being present. When you do, time will fly by. You will be totally engrossed in the moment and what you are doing. Discomfort and tension will naturally drop away as you allow your body to relax. Being present allows you to savor each moment and feel the vibrancy of each breath, each taste, each experience.

When hungry, eat your rice;
when tired, close your eyes.
Fools may laugh at me,
but wise men will know what I mean.

—*Lin Chi*

I'LL BE BACK

"I'll tell you a story about my teacher that I think you'll like," Gurucharan said. "Yogi Bhajan was walking with his teacher in India. It was very hot out that day, so they stopped to rest under the shade of a tree. After a time his teacher rose to continue their walk. But when Yogi Bhajan tried to join him, his teacher told him to stay. 'Climb up in the tree and wait until I get back.' So he did as his teacher instructed.

"Now, things in India are a little different than in this country. Some methods would be considered brutal here, but I'm just telling you the story. So Yogi Bhajan is up in the tree, and waiting and waiting. An hour passes, no teacher. A few hours pass, no teacher. Now to stay in a tree for a short time is no problem. But after a while, you have to go to the bathroom, you get a cramp, you get tired and want to sleep. It's tough. His teacher didn't come back for three days."

"Three days?" I said.

Gurucharan nodded. "And when he did, there was no, 'How are you? Did you do okay? Oh, you are so patient to have passed this test.' He just said, 'Okay, come on now.' So that's his perspective as a teacher. You can't just talk about patience. You can not just understand it intellectually. You have to understand it with your whole body."

"Just like martial art teachers had their students sweep floors or carry wood for two or three years before they taught them anything," I said.

"Exactly. To tame their monkey mind."

"There's that monkey again," I said.

"So to talk about taming the monkey mind is one thing. It's a good story and therefore easy to remember. But just to talk about it won't change anything. You have to discipline your mind and your body in order to understand."

"That makes sense. It's like you know what to do

but even though the spirit is willing, the flesh is weak."

"Right! So we have to build up the flesh, the physical aspect of ourselves. If we get too intellectual, then we are not using our full power."

Gurucharan looked thoughtful for a moment.

"Which brings me to another story about Yogi Bhajan, except this time it was me in the tree, metaphorically speaking...Now, you know I love to read."

That's an understatement. Gurucharan is a very intellectual person. He was almost done with a Ph.D. in mathematics before switching fields of study. Then he got a Master's degree in education, and a Ph.D. in psychology. He is a truly brilliant man, always reading about physics, chemistry, physiology, the brain, anything.

"So," Gurucharan continued, "he told me, 'No books for one year.'"

Gurucharan's eyebrows raised in remembered disbelief.

"A whole year? None? And he said, 'None.' But what about...? 'None.' And I did. I went a whole year without reading any books. I accomplished the task. At the end of the year I went to see Yogi Bhajan on a Saturday morning. He was relaxing reading the *New York Times*. He saw me and said, 'Come here. I have a little task. A treat for you.'

"He was dangling a very thick book by its edge, swinging it back and forth in the air. Tempting me. I snatched it up. He told me to read the entire thing, cover to cover, and report on it in twenty minutes.

"This book, mind you, was over four hundred pages long, on neuropsychology and a theory on brain functions. I sat down and concentrated with every fiber. I almost photographed each page in my mind as I ran through the chapters. Twenty minutes was up in the blink of an eye.

"'Report!' Yogi Bhajan said.

"So I began to explain the book, its theories, its flaws, and where I thought the author should go. He kept reading his paper the whole time, but once, when I paused, he gave me a look that let me know he was listening intently to every word. After about fifteen minutes he put down his paper and asked me a question.

"'Did you learn all that from that book? From reading?'

"Sir, I couldn't actually read all the words in twenty minutes, but I could read its heart.

"Yogi Bhajan smiled and said to me 'You have the ability to know something just by touching it. You pull the knowledge from it. That is your true intelligence. It was only clouded by too much intellect and attachment to that pleasure. Now read whatever you want, but read with the light of your heart.'"

I smiled. It was a good story, and a great lesson.

"So he pushed me to tap my intuition and trust my intelligence by countering the ego attachment to intellectual thinking. A teacher's test is rarely just a test. It also opens the door to a place within to develop."

One day a reporter waited at a train station in hopes of interviewing the great leader "Mahatma" Gandhi. He wanted to write a story for his paper. Try as he might, though, he was unable to get close to him. The throngs of people prevented him from getting near enough to grab the leader's attention.

Gandhi boarded the train. He sat down at a window seat and waved to the crowd as the train pulled away from the station. Desperate for at least a quote, the reporter raced alongside the tracks.

"Gandhi ji. Please, tell me your message so I can share it with the people," he shouted as he ran to keep up. Gandhi scribbled something on a piece of paper and handed it to the reporter.

It read, "My life is my message."

THE THIRD KEY

ON YOUR MARK,
GET CENTERED,
GO!

If a man wishes to be sure of the road he treads on,
he must close his eyes and walk in the dark.

—*St. John of the Cross*

I love the phrase: "Knowing what to do and doing what you know are two different things."

How many times have we seen world-class athletes, who have trained their entire lives, fall apart in the crucial moment, bungling movements they have done thousands of times? They knew what to do. Absolutely knew it. But why didn't they follow through and do what they knew?

They'll say they were a little off, or that they couldn't get it together.

Or what about in school. Have you ever been in a situation where you knew the answer, had memorized it, studied the material, but when it came time for the test, you froze up? You couldn't remember?

This has happened to us all in different situations. If we are not centered, we will not be able to do what we may have spent a lifetime perfecting, and all our practice will be for naught.

By centered, I don't mean some kind of ethereal supreme calm. Being centered means being in the moment, with your body and your breath and your spirit all together. It means understanding your emotions and not being controlled by them. We all know that these things are connected, but sometimes forget that if the body is affected by the emotions, then the emotions can be affected by the body. Or if our minds are distracted, then so will our bodies be. For example, if I said that right now there was someone behind a curtain who was depressed, and I would give you a thousand dollars to describe their posture, you could do it, couldn't you?

Where would their head be? Down, right? What about their breathing? It would be shallow, wouldn't it? Would they be sitting up straight with their shoulders back, or would they be slumped over? Slumped, no doubt. And, if I asked, you could probably describe what their facial expression would be, too.

So how do you know this? How come you can describe someone who is depressed with such a high degree of accuracy?

One of the things Tony Robbins was fond of saying is that "Motion creates emotion", that emotion is impacted by how we move, breathe, and gesture.

Masters have learned how to manage their emotions to a very high degree. Certainly they have and experience emotions, but they are not controlled by them. What I was interested in was how they manage to do this on a consistent basis. Specifically, I wanted to know how they were able to tame their monkey mind. What I discovered is that they all had some method of centering themselves every day, some physical routine that they used. The results are truly powerful.

I used to do this on a smaller scale in my personal development seminars all the time. I would ask my students, "Do something really silly with me for a moment, will you? Slump down in your chairs for me."

Generally everyone in the group would do as I asked.

"Good. I'm glad to see you had to move," I'd say, a sure-fire joke. "Now, with your head slumped down, make your breathing real shallow for a moment. That's it, real shallow, with your head slumped down. Now make sure you have a slack expression on your face, and keep your body and breathing the same."

I would watch to make sure everyone was doing it.

"Now, without changing anything, staying the exact same way, think about something that usually excites you."

A couple people started to laugh, but most didn't. When I asked how many of them felt excited, only the couple that started to laugh raised their hands. The others reported feeling negative or neutral at best.

"Now those of you that felt good, you changed your body, either by laughing or smiling, which changes what you are doing with your face, and your breathing. The rest of you couldn't get excited by the thought because the thought alone wasn't what made you experience excitement. It was the thought plus the corresponding body posture and breathing that made you feel a certain way."

Then I'd get them to try something that was a bit more fun. "Shake your body out. Shake, shake, shake. Really move it around." I'd have my sound technician in the back of the room crank up some music. Once the energy in the room started to go through the roof, I'd say, "Now sit up in your chair with tons of energy. Sit up straight, with your shoulders back, breathing fully, look at the ceiling, and put a big, stupid, silly grin on your face."

Most everyone would start to laugh.

"Now, keeping that grin, shoulders back, breathing fully, think about something that gets you depressed."

Again the laughter.

"Come on, get depressed, but keep smiling, get really depressed, but keep on smiling. Come on, work at it. I want you to get really depressed."

By this time everyone was cracking up.

"Okay, come back down, unless you want to stay there. Now, what happened? How many of you got depressed?"

No one raised their hand.

It was pretty simple. As simple as it was, though, it was also so powerful. That's because our bodies send a signal to our brains on how to feel. Manic depressives who have to take a drug to change how they feel have done these kind of exercises for just twenty minutes a day and, in some cases, were able to go completely off their medication. Why? Because the most powerful drugs you have are in your body.

What I came to realize as I studied with these masters is that they all had learned to tap into the power of their bodies to control and master their lives. It was not by chance, then, that they were able to act and react in certain ways. They had trained their bodies and minds using distinct methods in order to achieve the kind of results that they desired.

Being centered is the third key, and every master has a way of centering themselves. Once you know your mark, get centered before you go.

THE STRENGTH OF THE EARTH

"Watch here," Sifu Fong said as he took what seemed to be a normal, relaxed, standing posture. He then called up two of the biggest and strongest guys in the room, both weight lifters. One of them, a guy named Bill Gebhardt, was an assistant defensive coach for the Penn State football team. They dwarfed Sifu Fong as they stood next to him.

"Push my hand," Sifu Fong said playfully to Bill, extending his arm.

Bill grabbed Sifu Fong's hand with both of his and attempted to push him over.

Sifu Fong relaxed his body completely. It looked as if he poured himself into the ground. He grinned as Bill turned red with effort. While Bill was still straining mightily, he lifted one of his legs and wiggled the fingers on his hand that Bill had hold of. His arm was completely relaxed.

"You too, sir," he said to the other volunteer. He joined Bill and pushed right along with him. Their feet slipped on the gymnasium floor as they pushed harder and harder.

Sifu Fong just laughed as he called two more men to join them. All four men pushed for all they were worth, but Sifu Fong didn't move an inch.

"Okay, take a break," he said to the four. "Go relax, you look all tired out." He laughed as they walked back to the group, shaking their heads in disbelief.

Sifu Fong pointed to Bill. "This isn't about strength. I'm not stronger than him. No way. He is much stronger than me. But when I relax into the ground, he is pushing into it. Look here."

He called Bill back over.

He took his stance again, but this time his body was tight, every muscle rigid and contracted.

"If we go muscle to muscle, mine against his, I'll lose."

Bill tried once again, and this time he pushed Sifu Fong back fairly easily.

"See? But if I relax and sink into the ground, then he is pushing against that. And there's a saying in China. 'No one is smarter than the heavens, no one is stronger than the earth.' So let your partner push against the ground. Let him fight himself. Don't fight against him. Don't use your muscles. I don't have much muscle, just bones, so I have to use them."

As he walked around checking on his students, he invited me to try and push him. It was like trying to move a boulder.

Although he probably weighs no more than one hundred and forty pounds, he might as well have weighed one thousand and forty pounds. I have never felt that kind of power and rootedness before, even when I practiced with guys that weighed over two hundred and fifty pounds in college wrestling.

He invited us to try it with each other. To my surprise, relaxing and sinking into the ground actually worked. My partner pushed as hard as he could on me, and I didn't budge, nor did he when we switched.

"This is the most important, to be grounded and centered. Everybody wants to practice all the fancy stuff," he said as he performed an intricate technique, hands a mere blur to my dazzled eye. "Right?"

We all answered yes.

He waved his hands. "That won't matter if you don't get the grounding. The power is not in your hands. It's in the centering, coming up from the ground through your legs. It's energy stored in your waist. Move from your lower diaphragm. The dan tien. That's where the power is.

"Understand? Like a little kid that doesn't want to be picked up. You ever try that? This little kid might weigh twenty pounds, but he sinks down and you can't lift him. He feels like a hundred pounds, and you think, 'What the hell is this kid eating? How did he get so heavy?'

"It's something we automatically do. But later on, when we get older, we think we're smart so we try to use our muscles, just our force. It's better to relax. Use what you were born with. Just relax, don't fight against him. Let him fight himself. Redirect his energy into the ground. Practice that first. Once you have that then you can go on. Until you get that, nothing else will matter."

A few months later, in a private session, Sifu Fong elaborated on the same concept. I was having trouble with a particular technique.

"I understand intellectually what to do," I said. "I tell my students the same thing. My body hasn't quite caught on yet, though."

He nodded. "It's not just something for your mind to grasp. You have to understand it with your entire body. There's a Chinese proverb that says, 'Hear, and I forget. See, and I remember. Do, and I understand.'

"So you can hear the words, and see someone else do it, but you have to do it yourself to fully understand. You can't just see the move. All these people want me to make a video, but I tell them that a video can't convey the feeling. All you see is the movement, so your brain will know where to put your arm. But the feeling is something you can't get by watching. You have to feel it by working with someone else who knows. You can't separate your mind from your body. If you think about hitting, then your body will tense. If you think about fighting, then you can't relax, no way."

I nodded. "I have found that out the hard way."

He smiled. "You have to work on your centering. Once you are centered, then you can control the mind. And when you discipline your mind, you can control your body. Without control of your mind and body, you can never master yourself. This isn't just for martial arts. If you aren't centered, you will get knocked off base very easily. You will get frustrated by the littlest things, you won't even be able to do those things you know well. It's not what you know, it's what you do."

"So how do you get centered, Sifu? Just sink down?"

Sifu Fong nodded. "It's both your mind and your body." He stood in front of me and relaxed all of the muscles of his upper body. His feet were square to mine, about shoulder width apart, and his toes were pointed inwards. He extended his hand and asked me to push.

I did, with all my strength, to no avail.

"So you tense up?" I asked.

He shook his head and got himself centered again. He took my hand and placed it on his abdomen at the level of his waistband.

"Go ahead and push."

I did, but my hand kept going. There was absolutely no resistance at all. My hand kept going in as the muscles of his stomach folded over on top of my fingers. His back looked arched, like a cat's.

I was amazed.

"Don't give them any resistance, nothing to fight against. Sink down and relax."

I shook my head in disbelief. "I'll have to work on that one, sir."

He worked with me for a few minutes, after which he said, "Just keep at it. Being centered is so important. More important than the movements. Once you can center yourself, then the progress will come. But if you don't, your success will be temporary because something will come and knock you off your balance."

"Yes, sir," I said. I committed to practicing centering.

"Do it every day. Start your day like that. Then go about your day, no problem."

How can you think and hit at the same time?

—Yogi Berra

THE POWER OF THE BREATH

"How long can you go without food?" Gurucharan asked the group. We were sitting in the recreation room of St. Mary's Church in Cambridge, Massachusetts, for his Thursday night Kundalini Yoga class.

"About two months," a woman answered.

Gurucharan nodded. "And water? How long can you go without water?"

The same woman responded. "A few days, maybe ten at the most."

"What about air?" he asked. "Only a few minutes before you have brain damage and die. So when we exercise, what should be the most important?"

"Breathing," we answered.

"Now we can talk about the monkey mind, and letting things go. It's easy to say, but harder to do, right? It's possible to discipline the mind by thought alone, but why not tap into the power of the breath? In all cultures and many disciplines people use the power of the breath. In Zen, in martial arts, in religion, through chanting or songs.

"Yoga means union, between you and the infinite. In the old classic writings there are eight steps or stages to the practice of yoga. The first limb or stage is the yamas and niyamas, which are the Do's and Don'ts of how to live a lifestyle. So to practice that first stage, we become vegetarians, eat lighter, and become concerned with our neighbors and ecology."

I looked around the room and noticed student nodding their heads and taking notes.

"The next step is the asanas, or the postures that most people think of when they think of yoga. Now, in the U.S. there is suddenly every kind of body work imaginable because we're finally saying, 'Oh, the body isn't a dead thing! The body has energy. Oh my God, we've discovered it!'" Gurucharan rolled his eyes in amazement, shaking his head as if he couldn't believe it was possible that people had taken so long to finally admit that the body is alive.

"Then, slowly, we discover pranayama, breath work. Here, in New Age circles, breath work is a big discovery. It's 'holotropic', it's 'rebirthing,' it's this, it's that, like we just invented breathing, folks. Been around forever. In almost every traditional culture. In fact, we're doing a lot of research with Harvard on meditation and breath. And a lot is already being documented; things that the yogis have known for years, scientists in the West are just figuring out."

I already knew about some of the research. It illustrated how changing the rate of breathing dramatically alters the brain waves to a state that resembles a deep state of relaxation but also one of alertness. It was really quite fascinating.

"When you breathe normally, the rate is sixteen to twenty breaths per minute for the average adult. In certain chants, songs, or even katas, you know, the forms in martial arts, in all these things, the rate of breathing slows down dramatically. When it gets down to below eight per minute, you feel terrific. Your brain wave patterns alter and resemble a state of relaxed alertness. When you get down to four breaths per minute, inhaling and exhaling being one cycle, then your body's ability to heal itself goes up dramatically. When you get to one per minute or less, you are in a place of absolute bliss."

Gurucharan smiled and closed his eyes. He didn't open them for over a minute, but kept up the smile the entire time.

"With that pattern of breathing, you go into a meditative state. Your thoughts will come. You can't stop them, it's impossible, but your reaction to that thought changes. Right?"

Gurucharan continued his description.

"At first you have a thought, and you have a body

reaction to that thought. You picture someone you don't like and think, 'I can't stand her,' and your stomach tightens and your face flushes. Your heartbeat quickens and adrenaline flows into your bloodstream."

Gurucharan scrunched up his face in mock anger.

"Then, later on, as you continue to meditate, you have the same thought. But now your reaction is diferent. You don't get angry. You simply notice the picture. 'Oh, that's nice. It's that person, again. What an odd style she has.' But no body reaction," he said, shaking his head.

"Then, by and by, you see that person in real life and can deal with her as she is, without the emotional attachment. Without that anger you can come from a state of compassion. Perhaps this person is someone who could use some understanding. So it's not the event or the person that changes, it is your perception and reaction to that person."

Maybe he saw our faces looked a little doubtful, so he switched to an example we could all relate to. "Your child spills the milk. One day you take it in stride and say, 'Okay, come on, let's clean it up.' Then another day you start yelling, 'How many times have I told you not to…!'"

I knew that example was all too real for me.

"Your mother knew all about breath control. Didn't she tell you when you are angry to take a few deep breaths? Now we have to spend millions of dollars to prove what your mother knew a long time ago. The quickest way to change how your mind works is by changing the way you breathe. It's not too sexy, but it's true.

"So the masters are not supernatural people with the inborn patience of a saint. They are people who do their sadhana, their practice, every day. They use their meditation and breath to control their emotions to open up to the spirit to have that yoga, that union. Then you can have the inner peace. But you have to do the work first."

I had the opportunity to apply what Gurucharan had taught when I returned to Rochester a few days later. Although I had been meditating in the morning, and had enjoyed very positive results, I would sometimes get knocked off center during the day. Specifically at the end of the day. Well, specifically at the end of the day when I came home to garbage that wasn't taken out, chores that weren't done, or kids whose favorite pastime seemed to be arguing with each other. My hard-earned state of centeredness would quickly dissipate, and I would find myself yelling, and then feel guilty.

I came to realize that my "blissful state" didn't hold up through the entire day, especially when I came home tired. So I began doing something that had a profound impact on my ability to handle these types of situations.

When I was about five minutes from returning home, I would practice long, deep breaths in the car. Sometimes I would pull over on the side of the street, before I got to my house, and spend two or three minutes in silent meditation. Just getting re-centered on my priorities: being loving towards Jessie and the kids, not being a manager of chores.

After a few minutes, I would feel great. Refreshed and centered, looking forward to seeing my family. If there was a chore that wasn't done, or arguing, I felt relaxed and dealt with it calmly. I could also be much more supportive and encouraging towards my kids.

And I noticed that once I quit nagging them, they began to do the chores more on their own. And if they forgot, as soon as they saw me they would say, "Oh, I forgot to do this. Let me do it right away."

"Yeah, sounds good. But first give me a hug." And it was great. Just a subtle shift in what I did, but it paid significant dividends in how I acted and how my children reacted.

In this very breath that we take now lies
the secret that all great teachers try to tell us.

—*Peter Matthiessen*

A BALANCING ACT

Sil lum tao is the first form in Wing Chun Kung Fu. Translated, it means "small thought" or "little idea". As Sifu Fong is fond of saying, "If you don't get the little idea, you won't get the big one."

In one part of the form you have to shoot out both of your arms to the sides. You start with the left hand on top of the right, then whip them out, and then bring them back in with the right hand on top of the left. During class one evening we were focusing on practicing this move.

"Who knows why you do that? Start one way then come back the other way?" Sifu Fong asked the class.

"To bring both hemispheres of the brain into balance," said one of the students.

"That's right. That guy's pretty smart. It's to use both sides, not just one. That way you're much stronger. Try it."

My partner pushed down on my arms. They were in what is called a double lan sao position. It looks like a block in football, elbows up at shoulder level, arms folded in front of your chest, except that in the lan sao the fingertips are in line with the ends of the forearms.

I thrust my arms out to the sides, and brought them back in. The first time I did it correctly. He pushed down and couldn't move them.

The next time I did the same thing, but came back placing the same hand on top. This time my partner pushed my arms down easily.

"No way," I exclaimed. "That's weird. Let me try again."

I did, with the same results. We switched, and the same thing happened with him.

"See, I don't want you to believe what I say automatically. Try it for yourself and see how it works. Did it work for you?" Sifu Fong asked as he came around to my partner and I.

"Yes, sir, it did."

"Your brain is the most powerful tool you have. But you need to make sure you are using the whole thing, not just half. You have to balance it out. That's why in the forms you always do both sides, and why there are twisting movements. A lot of it is *chi gong*, moving your body energy, or *chi*, around.

"Without balance you have no power."

A few months later, during a private lesson, he elaborated.

"Balance is physical. Like yin and yang. Look here." His hips and feet were shifted just slightly, so there was more weight on one leg. "This is my heavy leg. What is my hand on that side doing?"

It was in a position called *tan-sao* where his palm was turned up and extended in front of his chest.

"It's up," I said.

"Heavy or light?" he asked.

"Light."

"My other foot is light. Not too much weight," Sifu Fong said.

"And your other hand is down, heavy." It was in a position called *bong-sao*.

"See? Heavy and light, light and heavy. There has to be a balance all the time."

I shook my head and laughed in utter amazement at the depth that these simple movements contained.

"Pretty interesting, huh? So there is physical, but balance is more mental. It's paying attention. Like this."

He began the Wing Chun rolling hands exercise with me called *chi-sao*. From the outside, *chi-sao* looks like two people both grabbing on to a small invisible steering wheel at the same time, turning it one way, then the other. Your hands are extended and crossed over your partners.' Both people have one hand on the inside of the circle, and one on the outside. By rotating your arms and shoulders clockwise and counterclockwise, you roll the circle, first half a circle one way, and then back the other.

At the apex of the rolling, Sifu Fong exerted pressure onto my wrist where we were connected.

"Don't just think from point to point. From one," he said as he reached the point where we switched directions, "to two. Understand?"

"Yes, sir. I need to pay attention all the way through."

"Right. Not like this, one…two…one…two," he said in a robotic tone, applying staccato-like pressure at each turning point. "Like this, one aaannnnddddd two, aaannnnddddd one aaannnnddddd two." And I could feel his energy staying with mine this time, all the way through the circle.

"Like a waltz," I said.

"That's it exactly. You don't go from step to step, that's not the goal. It's to flow freely while going from step to step. Tune into the rhythm. Everything has a rhythm. Like breathing, in and out, in and out. Not just in, in, in! In! IN! IN!!! You'll explode."

I laughed.

"So balance is smooth, like rolling a ball. Pay attention all the time, not just from point to point. Be present at all times, pay attention at all times. Balance is physical," he said as he reviewed the points we had covered, "and it is mental."

"So develop both," I said.

"Develop both," he replied.

The notes I handle no better than many pianists.
But the pauses between the notes -
ah, that is where the art resides.

—Artur Schnabel

EXAMINE YOUR INTENT

Kodak was in the midst of some very challenging times. We were about to announce a down-sizing like none that had ever been experienced before. Since this was to impact people who had worked for the company for years, some of them their entire work life, it was particularly painful. The managers found it very difficult to make decisions which would impact their friends and colleagues whom they had known for years. I know I did.

I asked Jeff McLeod how he dealt with such tough issues.

"Whenever I make a decision, I try to think through the effects that decision will have. I know that some of the decisions I make won't be popular."

"Especially the ones we have to make now."

He nodded his head in agreement as he leaned back in his chair. "These are particularly difficult times. When faced with tough decisions like these, though, I always try to do what I know in my heart is the right thing to do. Even though it may impact some people negatively, I always strive to do what is right for the greater number of people. If the intent is right, then I will go ahead."

"I see."

"Like I said to you when you first came on board. You can make a mistake that costs a million dollars. I won't like it, but if your intent was good, then I'll stand behind you."

"Oh, I'm glad, because..."

Jeff laughed.

"Just kidding," I said. "Do you just know it's right? I mean, how do you get that sense?"

"Well, some comes from experience. I've been here for a long time. But it also comes from my quiet time. I have a routine, it's kind of a devotional time I put in every morning, at least I try to do it every morning, when I check my intent. I think about it. I think about my decisions in light of my intent and beliefs. If I know my decision's intent is right, then I just need to do it. If it's just an issue of courage, then I have to be strong and go do it. It's as simple as that."

You'll never go wrong doing what's right.

—Anonymous

KEEP UP AND YOU WILL BE KEPT UP

When I started working with Gurucharan promoting his seminars and workshops, one of the things that I noticed was lacking for his out-of town students was the availability of any kind of study materials that they could use to practice after he left.

So we decided to create a six-cassette audio tape series called *Happiness is Your Birthright.* We arranged to do the recording in downtown Boston on a Saturday morning, so my family and I left Rochester the night before to be there the next day. Jessie's parents had a place outside of Albany where she and the kids would stay while I drove on to Boston to make the eight a.m. taping.

That overnight drive was one of the longest in my life. A few weeks before, I had come down with bronchial-pneumonia. Thinking it was just a cold, I put off going to the doctor until just before the trip. When I finally broke down and went, my doctor gave me a prescription for an antibiotic, and I was told to take a double dose for the first two days to get the level in my bloodstream up.

About three hours into the trip I was struck with the worst stomach cramps I had ever experienced. I couldn't drive any longer, so Jessie took over as I lay on the floor of our minivan, curled up into a fetal position. It kept getting worse. I had Jessie pull the car over three times. The third time I lay down on the tarmac, praying that the pain would go away. It was snowing out. The temperature was below thirty, but I was sweating with only a light jacket on. Jessie, fearing that I might be having an allergic reaction to the medication, flagged down a state trooper.

I was rushed by ambulance to the emergency room of the nearest hospital where I was given an I.V. and a drug to make me vomit. After three hours there, my stomach felt a little better, but I still had a terrible cough and I was exhausted.

By the time we got to the farm it was past two. I had to be in Boston by eight, and it was still a three hour drive. As soon as my head hit the pillow my coughing spasms started again. I knew I wasn't going to get any sleep, so I drove to Boston that night.

I arrived around six, stopped and got some tea, and waited until the production studio opened. I must have looked like hell when I got there because everyone kept asking me if I was okay.

I somehow managed to make it through the day, but barely. By that evening, I was completely wiped out. After being up for more than thirty six hours, and running a temperature of a hundred and one, I was hoping that I would be able to sleep.

Gurucharan was going to visit a friend in Rhode Island, so he told me I could sleep in his room instead of on the couch where I usually stayed. As soon as I entered his room I felt calm and relaxed. It was very peaceful. To my great surprise, I was asleep in a matter of minutes.

The next morning I woke up feeling better than I had in weeks. There was no trace of a cough. Nothing. I had had bronchial-pneumonia before, and it took me about three or four months before I was feeling back to normal. This instant recovery was incredible. I couldn't believe it. I had to ask him about it.

The next week Gurucharan and I were relaxing in my living room. He had just driven in from Boston to do a two-day workshop in Rochester. Now was the time. I asked him what he thought had happened.

He downplayed it, but gave me at least this. "Can you pick up when someone is angry? Even if you don't know them?"

"Of course."

"What about scared? You can pick that up too, right?"

I said that I could.

"It's the same thing with positive or healing energy. You pick that up. Your body does too."

I told him I had read a lot of research about fear pheromones, or smells, that animals emit when they are frightened. If another animal comes into the room afterwards, they too panic because they pick up the scent, literally the smell of fear.

He nodded. "On the opposite end of the spectrum there are people who send out signals of peace. You like being around those kind of people. Animals pick it up too. Once I was in a park in Boston and all these birds and squirrels came right by me."

"Did you have food?" I said.

He shook his head. "Like a baby. Everyone wants to hold it and kiss it, even little kids. Why? Because the baby has such a great energy, everyone wants to be around it."

"You're right about that, sir."

"See, we tend to rely on our new brain too much," Gurucharan said.

"The new brain?"

"Yeah, the conscious mind. We forget the old brain that controls our reflexes and instincts. These are very powerful, and control a lot of things that our conscious minds don't understand."

As we were sitting and chatting, the oddest sensation came over me. As if I were floating. I felt peaceful, just like I had in his room.

Despite these feelings, I was skeptical. It seemed a little 'New Age-y' to me. I couldn't totally buy it or explain it, but I know what I felt. I told Gurucharan. He simply smiled.

"How do you keep so centered and peaceful?" I said.

"In the West we ask, 'Are the body and mind connected? Is it dualistic, or one?' But in the yogi's mind we say that there is a balance between the body, mind and spirit. It's not a static thing. If you don't develop the eighteen major muscle groups in your body, then when you come under stress and you can't rely on the physical level, your mind will come in to compensate. And it will start dumping in emotions, freak outs, commotions, and everything else because you don't have the physical stamina there."

I nodded my head, but wasn't sure where this answer was leading.

"Here we do something, then say, 'Well, I didn't mean it.' Haven't you seen those trials?"

Gurucharan began a mock conversation: "They say, 'You shot this person, didn't you?' 'Well, yeah I did, but I didn't really plan it to happen that way.' 'I see. But you did it, right?' 'Yeah, I did, but I didn't really mean to.' 'You went into their house, you shot them four times, but you didn't really mean it?' 'Yeah, that's right. I did it, but I'm not sure why, I couldn't stop myself.' It's really pretty fascinating, the excuses that we use."

I chuckled. "Crimes of passion."

"Exactly. See, here we talk about the body as if it is this unconscious, impulse-ridden, Freudian glut of snakes and weird dreams. But from a yogi's perspective, your body isn't something you try to control, or even sculpt and create to perfection."

"No buns of steel?" I asked.

Gurucharan laughed. "No buns of steel. More like nerves of steel. What good are buns of steel if your nervous system is weak? So in the East, truth doesn't mean knowing something intellectually. It means being in a mode of consciousness to be able to live a certain way."

"So your actions and intentions are one."

He nodded. "There isn't a thought, then a different action. They are one. It's all one substance. Like ice and water and steam, all the same thing, just different energy levels."

"Okay."

"So there are connections. In yoga we have chakras, seven energy centers. In China they teach about meridians that flow all over the body, so that doing something over here," he said as he pressed on the space between his thumb and forefinger, "has an effect up here." He pointed to his head.

"When you take a posture it is not just random. It is not aerobics or weight lifting to develop how you look. It is to develop you as a total person. For example, how do you think the posture of prayer came about?" He placed his hands together as in prayer.

"I've never really thought about it," I answered.

"Do you think it's random that all these people, from totally different cultures and religions, do the same thing?"

"Probably not, sir."

"What about chanting? We say 'ohhnnggg' in yoga, but monks say 'ohmmm,' and Christians say 'amen.' Jews, too, except they pronounce it 'oh-main.'"

I smiled. "That's true, I guess. I had never considered it that way before."

"So there are certain things that you can do with your body and mind and breath so that your actions are in accordance with your intentions. So that what you do with your body is what is in your heart."

"That's what yoga is all about," I said.

"Yes. But not everyone will be into yoga. It freaks some people out. That's okay. But at least people should be aware that there are certain ways to move your body to center and ground you. It's not magic. You just have to do it every day. Your sadhana. If you miss it, you mess up," Gurucharan said.

"I have to admit I get pretty cranky if I miss my workout."

"Right. The big thing is endorphins, now. The body's pharmacy. But people have known about these types of things for years. That's what *chi-gong* is in China. Other cultures have it. But in the West we only want to look good or train for physical results."

"You have to do that for some things, though."

"Of course, do the training for whatever kind of activity you need. I mean, if you play in the NFL you better lift weights."

"Meditating isn't going to cut it, huh?"

He laughed. "Not by itself. You have heard the phrase, "Before enlightenment, chop wood, carry water. After enlightenment, chop wood, carry water?"

"Yes, sir, many times."

"So you still have to do the regular stuff. Train and develop to be able to carry out your duties. But get yourself centered. It doesn't matter whether you choose yoga or chi-gong or some style of martial arts, even walking with a certain breath like our BreathWalk will do it. Prayer can do it, and so can meditation. Everyone can benefit from this mind body connection. A lot of people today think they can just do it by thinking positively."

"The power of positive thinking."

"Which is good. That helps too, but that alone is very tough. If you add in the breath and the body, then it makes it much easier to stay on course. That makes us centered. Once we get centered, it is easier to do what we need to do."

"That makes sense," I said.

"So just keep up. Do your centering exercises every day. Keep up, and you will be kept up."

Get up, set up and keep up.

—*Gurucharan Singh Khalsa*

THE FOURTH KEY

GO WITH WHAT COMES

To set up what you like against what you don't like,
this is the disease of the mind.

—Seng-T'san

One day a man's prize stallion ran off. All the people of the village said, "What a terrible thing."

But the wise man said, simply, "Perhaps."

Two days later the stallion returned with three beautiful mares. All the villagers exclaimed, "What good fortune!" to which the man said, "Perhaps."

In an attempt to break the mares the man's only son was thrown from one of the horses and broke his leg. The villagers bemoaned his fate, "What awful luck."

Once again the wise man said, "Perhaps."

The next week the elders of the village took all the young men to fight in a battle, but the wise man's son was spared because of his injury.

All the young men later died in that battle.

Maybe you have an experience that you can relate to this story. I know I do.

I must have replayed the sickening scene a hundred times in my head in the hours that followed. We weren't at the park more than five minutes before it happened.

Danny and David's cub scout troop was having its annual Winter Derby at a nearby park. It was a bright, sunny day. Snow had fallen the night before, making the conditions perfect for sledding. We loaded up the minivan with sleds and saucers and drove over anticipating a fun-filled day.

There were already a bunch of people there when we arrived. Parents and kids sledding down a couple of different hills. Rachel brought her friend Sarah along with her, and they decided to go down a hill together. After two trips down, they opted for another one.

I looked over. There were a few kids going down it, but there was an enormous oak tree near the bottom of the hill to one side. It seemed all right, but I gave them a stern warning just in case. "Now listen, girls. If you start going towards the tree, jump off, okay?"

"Okay," they assured me with the confident smiles

of nine year olds.

I don't know why I didn't go down there to make sure all the kids stayed clear of the tree. I guess I thought it was far enough away. And I figured if they needed to they could jump off.

They started down the hill. I couldn't believe it. They were heading right for the tree. At first I thought they would turn, but as they picked up speed I knew they were going to hit. My stomach gave a sickening lurch as I shouted for them to jump.

They barreled straight towards the oak. It looked like Rachel was trying to get out, but her feet were stuck. All I could think of was her head being smashed into the tree.

They smacked right into it. Rachel, who was in front, hit the tree with the full weight of both of them against her thigh.

My heart was in my throat as I raced down to her. She was in tears. Sarah seemed to be okay. I hoped that Rachel maybe had just a bad bruise, but one look at her leg told me otherwise. The impact had snapped the bone completely in half. It looked like she had two knees.

She ended up in traction for three weeks, and a half-body cast for close to five months. She turned out perfectly fine, but for the longest time I couldn't shake that image of how it might have turned out if she had been two inches to the left.

It was a terrible accident, and it could have been much worse. On the one hand she broke her leg, but on the other hand she was alive. Still it left my feelings in a tangle. Trying to sort out the guilty 'if only's' from my relief that she was healing and going to be okay. How can you judge a situation like that, where all the conclusions are relative to each other?

We often try to make sense of our world by categorizing things into black and white concepts of good and bad, night and day, true and false. We forget about the in between transitions from one opposite to the other. And that both elements are necessary. If it were always day, we would shrivel up and die from so much sunlight. If it were only night, there would be no photosynthesis, no warmth. We need both to exist.

A valuable lesson that the masters teach is going with the flow, a concept that I think is informed by the theory of yin and yang. Most people think that yin and yang describes opposites: white and black, male and female, strong versus weak, and so forth. And that is partly accurate. But it is not complete.

A better way to think of yin and yang is to think of a mountain peak that runs north and south. In the morning, when the sun first rises, the east side of the mountain is illuminated, and the west is in complete darkness. Later, around noon, both east and west sides are fully illuminated. During sunset, only the west side is illuminated while the east is darkened, then at night both side are blackened. At different times, both sides of the mountain are both bright and dark.

So the concept of yin and yang more accurately refers to the balance that is realized by taking into account the changing dynamics of life. What was once good may be bad, and what was once fortunate may turn out to be unlucky indeed. The trick, then, is not to judge, because one never knows what other forces may be acting in a given situation. And because everything is constantly changing, our job is to balance in between the opposites, not to rush to one extreme or the other. The Chinese have a saying: "Humanity is found between the heavens and the earth." Balance.

The fourth key is all about going with what comes, not judging. It is something that I believe we all wish we did better, a key component along the path of mastery.

KEEP THINGS IN PERSPECTIVE

"How do you roll with the punches, so to speak? When things get tough, you always seem to maintain a positive attitude. How do you do that?" I asked Jeff McLeod during a breakfast meeting one morning.

"I guess I try to keep a perspective on things. Back in my office I keep a piece of cotton on my shelf. Most people don't notice it. But it reminds me of how things could be. See, when I was a kid, both my parents worked. And in the summer, so did my brother and two sisters. I was the youngest, and since I didn't want to stay home alone, I went with my brother and sisters.

"We had a job working on a farm picking cotton. From six in the morning to five at night. All day, and it was hot."

"I can imagine."

"No sob story. I didn't have to work, but I did. By the end of the day we were beat. So when things get tough here, I just look at the cotton and think, could be worse," he said laughing.

"That's a good perspective to have."

"Well, like in Malaysia where I was for a few years as a manager. One day a guy came running in saying that a cobra was in the warehouse, and they couldn't ship anything because of the snake."

"So what happened?" I asked.

"Oh, we got it out. But when I think about the problems there, not just the snake, but the poverty, I think: we don't have any problems here compared to that. And the problems we do have give us the opportunity to grow. If we didn't have any problems, we would never grow. So I don't see them as bad or negative, but more as a chance to learn and get better."

Barn's burnt down, now I can see the moon.

—Masahide

"Look without seeing. Does that make sense?"

Sifu Fong called one of the students out to the middle of the floor.

"Now look straight into my eyes. Keep looking." Sifu Fong raised both arms out away from his body, and put up two fingers of his right hand and three of his left.

"Keep looking at my eyes, how many fingers do I have up?"

The student hesitated. "Uhh…two?"

"On both hands?"

"I think so. I'm not sure."

Sifu Fong began wiggling the toes of his left foot. "How about my feet. Which one is moving?"

The student smiled. "I can't tell, sir."

Sifu Fong grinned. "Okay, now look at the center of my chest. Now how many fingers am I holding up?"

This time the student gave the right answer.

"And which foot is moving?"

Again, the correct response.

"See where his chin is?" he asked the rest of us. "Down into his body more where it protects his throat. If you look up, guess where your head goes?"

"Up," I said.

"Right. Now I didn't say look at my foot. If you do that I'll give it to you." Francis Fong kicked at his head with no effort at all, missing his face by a hair's breadth.

"You need to look, but don't see. Hear, but don't listen. Do you know what I mean? Like a good cop. They'll stop you for speeding, and you say, 'Oh, sorry officer. Was I going a little fast? Well, see that's because…,' and you go on and tell them this big, long story.

"All the while he's writing out a ticket, nodding his head, 'Uh huh…yep…sure…I understand, these things happen.' Then he gives you the ticket anyway.

"But you think, 'Oh, he's such a nice cop, he

listened to me!'"

I laughed as Sifu Fong acted his entire story out.

"But you still get the ticket, right? So be like the cop. Look, but don't get hooked. Like the cop, he listens, but it doesn't affect him. So in Wing Chun it's the same thing. If you get caught up too much in one thing, if you over react or over commit, you'll get caught."

In our next private session I asked him if he would elaborate on this topic.

"In Hong Kong, teachers don't look at your form to see how good you are. They check your *chi-sao*, your sticking hands, because they can see how you react."

Sifu Fong put his hands out away from his body in front of him, and I did the same, interlocking our hands in the starting position of *chi-sao*.

"So, we start out with rolling hands, going slow, testing." He pushed through which forced me to react to his movements.

"Good. So then, once you begin to get that, we go to *poon-sao*." He pushed forward with the full force of his grounded frame, propelling me back five steps. Just as I began to recover from that he yanked me forward so quickly and powerfully that I nearly fell to the floor. I felt like a rag doll, helplessly being moved back and forth.

"*Poon-sao* means testing, questioning. To see what you're made of."

Not much, I thought, as I got tossed around the room.

"In *chi-sao* don't be anxious. Everyone wants to hit all the time, but..." He shook his head.

"Don't worry about it," I said.

He nodded. "Don't worry about it. If you over-react with one hand, then your other one will be weak." He pushed down on one of my arms, pinning it against my body. He quickly collapsed the other one as well. His one hand was holding both my arms, leaving his other hand free to hit me with.

"See? One hand against two. I'll win every time, unless you grow a third arm. If you do, I don't want to fight anymore."

I laughed. Even with three arms I didn't stand a chance.

"So never over commit. Test your partner, sense the situation. See how he reacts, then go with him. He is like the road, and you are the car. Go with what comes to you, immediately, without thought or reservation."

"Yes, sir."

We continued *chi-sao*. Within a minute, I over reacted to his forward thrust and pushed too far with my hand.

"Ah, Jim, see? Too much," he said as his hand circled under mine and came up from the outside to lightly touch my open face.

"Whatever you do will come back to you. If you push hard, you will get hit hard. So if I push hard on you, how much do you give back?"

"The same amount," I said.

"Right," he said loudly. "The same. Give what you get. There's a saying in Wing Chun. It says, 'Stay with what comes, follow as it retreats, thrust forward as the hand is freed.'

"Be like water. It surrounds but does not contain. But you have to have the mind to do that, too. Not just the body. Don't judge. Don't think about good or bad. As soon as you do you are stopping your mind. You are labeling."

I understood intellectually but I knew it would take a while before my body did what my mind knew.

"Nothing is all good or all bad. No one has only good days or only bad days. It's all the same. Just go with what comes to you, then you can relax. Okay?"

I agreed, and kept concentrating on the *chi-sao*.

"Don't over react to things. Stay centered and balanced. Practice your grounding and balance. Practice *chi-sao* with your eyes closed. After a while you will find that you always have that balance, that grounding. That way, you can handle any problem, no problem. Your practice will help you to develop these attributes in your every day interactions."

The way is not difficult, only there
must be no wanting or not wanting.

—*Chao-Chou*

THE FLOW

I have never heard Dan Inosanto speak an unkind word about anyone, even people who have maligned and misrepresented him. Nor does he speak ill of any martial art system. I think that his humility and non-judgmental attitude is at the heart of what allows him to flow so smoothly from one art to another, from one position to another with such effortless ease that it leaves any onlooker in absolute awe.

"Like everyone, obviously I have a preference for some styles or systems over others. But I can honestly say that I have respect for and have found something I like in every system or style I have trained in. In my personal training I find that I flow readily and easily, without a conscious thought process, from system to system. The more your cross-train, and the more open you are, the more you will find similarities in different systems and styles."

I generally am left in the dust when he starts flowing. He'll be demonstrating, and say something like, "Here's how they would attack in Kali, then if he moves back, I can go into this lock from Silat." Then in an instant he'll move to something else. "And then this is from Wing Chun," and on and on. The genius of his movement is not in knowing so many systems but in being able to integrate them into a unique whole. Rather than letting the style determine his next movement, he can integrate what he knows to such a degree that each move comes from within him and is not a mere reproduction of something memorized.

"The ability to flow from one situation to another, from long range, to middle range, to close quarters or ground attack is useful in the real world. You need to have those skills.

"If you are forced to fight, and left with no alternative, you should use anything and everything you have learned, from any system or style you have studied. If it will save you, don't try to stay within one style because it has the press of being the superior or ultimate art."

As all my teachers were constantly telling me, I had to learn again that it is only in the moment of confrontation, of decision making, or just of being with another human being whom I love that I can know what it is that will be required of me. Only in that moment will I be able to choose what is best for me regardless of hype or outside pressures.

> There is nothing good nor bad,
> only thinking makes it so.
>
> —*William Shakespeare*

SEE WITH YOUR HEART

We practiced rolling hands, *chi-sao*, for the entire hour and a half. By the end of the session, my arms were exhausted and my forearms ached down to the marrow, but my spirits were high. As we were walking out of the academy, Sifu Fong added a few thoughts.

"*Chi-sao* is a good exercise because it teaches you not to judge. If you judge in *chi-sao*, focus on an instant in time instead of looking at the entire person, you will get killed, make sense? In *chi-sao* you develop your intuition through sensitivity. You don't think what's right to do, you feel it."

"I'm finding that out, sir," I said. I knew that mastering *chi-sao* was a lifelong process. I would always have to keep working at it.

"You need to develop that sensitivity, your intuition, so that you don't rely on your mind so much. You know, the mind can be evil or an angel. It always wants this and that. It judges and criticizes. It will take snapshots of people, representing a moment in time, and pin them with a label of good or bad.

"But haven't we all had periods when someone could have taken our picture and labeled us as bad, when we knew that in our hearts we are good people just having a bad day?"

I agreed with him.

"If you let yourself be ruled by your mind, you'll go crazy. Better to let your heart rule you," he said. He placed his hand over the middle of his chest. "You'll never be misled by the heart."

It is only with the heart that one can see rightly;
what is essential is invisible to the eye.

—Antoine De Saint-Exupery

THE FIFTH KEY

PRACTICE

There is no fixed teaching.
All I can provide is an appropriate medicine
for a particular ailment.

—Bruce Lee

I once read a book in which the author sat next to the Dallas Cowboys' Coach, Tom Landry, on a plane. They got to talking, and the author, an expert on peak performance, asked Coach Landry what was the most important thing to know about developing skills.

"Focus on one thing at a time," he answered.

So many times, in an effort to get optimal results, we try to do everything at once. We try to rush things. But what actually happens is that we generally end up getting frustrated, and what little progress we make is fleeting, or temporary at best.

So the masters teach us to take our time. Go slow, and master the fundamentals. Don't look for progress to come too quickly. Be open to and ask for honest feedback, not false praise. All the masters that I know, in every field, invite feedback. They ask for it. Regardless of how well they are doing, they always ask people to help them get better. They know that we have trouble seeing our own weaknesses, so they constantly ask others to be their mirror. And then they thank them.

A friend of mine once said, "You know, if a martial arts teacher doesn't like you, they will simply ignore you. They will refuse to teach you."

"What if they hate you?" I asked.

"Even worse. They'll tell you you're doing a good job."

With this fifth key you'll see how the masters teach. It's one thing to practice. That's a given. But how you practice in the path of mastery is just as important as what you practice.

For years I trained by building up my strength. That's a fine training goal, except that I was already strong, both physically and in my personality. So, in effect, I was spending the majority of my time simply reinforcing behaviors that were already well developed.

But what if my most significant developmental

needs were in the areas of yielding, sensitivity and patience? My workout wouldn't really be developing those areas. Now, I could develop those characteristics in other ways, surely, but here's the catch.

How do we tend to act under stress? Do we generally flow directly into our newly learned behaviors? No. We fall back into our old routines, especially under periods of stress. So, let's say I decide to develop my sensitivity and patience by meditating and gardening. And, in the meantime, I keep weight lifting, measuring my progress through more repetitions and always pressing my maximum weight. Despite the added activities, I am still having a physical workout that emphasizes pushing through, and sweating it out. So if, in the past, the way I always got results was to push harder, and in my new regimen I am still training that way, then guess what I will do when under stress? Not hard to figure out.

If I train physically in the same manner, then I am conditioning my body to follow the same old principle. While that type of training is very good for persistence and discipline and blasting through stuff, which is definitely needed at times, it won't help me to develop in other areas. The only way I will develop sensitivity and patience on a physical level is to practice them on a physical level in a way that integrates them into the activity in which I want to be sensitive and relaxed.

Things like meditating and taking time in my life to garden and have relaxation are essential. But I had to learn to train not just my mind, but also my body to react in the ways that I desired. I had to unlearn a lot, and relearn that there are other ways to succeed. In fact, what the masters were showing me was that the short term blast through mentality wasn't it.

I had to go back and reconstruct a foundation that I was in too much of a hurry to build the first time around.

1,000 REPETITIONS

"Okay, time," Guro Dan called as the buzzer sounded. Someone shut off the ever-present music as we hustled back to the middle of the gym.

"Do you know it takes about a thousand repetitions of a movement before it gets imbedded into your muscle? It's called muscle memory. That seems like a lot, doesn't it?

"Maybe if you're really good it will only take you 950. But what that means is that you have to drill that movement 1,000 times before you can do it automatically. So you start with a single movement, and you drill it. Over and over."

He picked up a rattan stick and practiced swinging it in a single, swift motion over and over. He added another movement after the first, and repeated the combination about a dozen times.

"Then you add in a combination, and keep drilling it. Then you switch and add another piece in."

He again demonstrated what he was talking about.

"Now the trick is not to rush. Take your time and do it properly. Practice doesn't make perfect. Practice makes permanent. If you are doing it incorrectly, you are going to imbed that poor technique into your muscles. So take your time and get it right."

I remember watching Guro Dan train in Muay Thai with Ajarn Chai, his teacher. Even though I was supposed to be concentrating on what I was doing, I couldn't help but steal a few glances at him. While I and most of the rest of the group were blasting the pads as hard as we could, Guro Dan was going at a slow pace with a minimum of force. When I felt like I was about to vomit from exertion, he was taking his time, focusing on correct form and proper positioning. I felt like a kid huffing and puffing to keep up with an older brother who with long easy strides was slowly but surely leaving me in the dust.

"The second thing to work on is your attitude. See, if you get ticked off because you didn't master it on your third try, then chances are pretty good that you're not going to make it to a thousand," he said. So I turned my eyes back to my own focus mitt and, slowly and surely, began to practice again.

The teacher, if indeed wise,
does not bid you enter the house of their wisdom,
but leads you to the threshold of your own mind.

—*Kahlil Gibran*

DON'T FORGET TO HAVE FUN

When Francis Fong accepted me as an apprentice instructor, one requirement was that I had to have a minimum of twenty hours of training with him every year to keep my certification. Luckily for me, my work took me down to Atlanta on occasion and I could give myself the special treat of a private lesson with Sifu.

This time, we were practicing a new movement, one that I was having a bit of trouble with. He suggested that we take a little break.

"If you have fun while you practice, then you are more likely to keep up and continue. You'll be willing to devote the time that it takes to get good. It takes a lot of time and a lot of hits," Sifu Fong said.

"How many times do you think I've been hit in the face?"

"Probably a lot," I answered, even though I had difficulty envisioning that.

"Of course. Why do you think I look like this?" he said with a smirk. "Don't laugh too much, now."

I suppressed my grin. "No, sir. Not at all funny."

"So what would happen if each time I got hit I thought, 'Oh no. I'm no good. I'll never amount to anything.' Do you think I'd still want to practice?"

"No, sir."

"Of course not. I would get down on myself and would feel lousy. Then I wouldn't feel good about practicing, then I would dread it, and then I would quit."

That had happened to a lot of people I knew. People who had a lot of innate talent but put too much pressure on themselves.

"Go lighter. Take it easy."

I agreed that I would, though it was something I have had to work very hard to remind myself consistently.

"In Wing Chun it's different than a lot of other

martial arts. In practice, back in Hong Kong, people would stop and take a break. Have some water or tea. The masters would sometimes drink wine before they did sticking hands, *chi-sao*."

"So I should drink before coming to class, Sifu?" I asked not at all seriously.

"Yeah, sure, no problem," he replied in just the same way.

"Why is that, though, Sifu?" I said.

"So you can develop your sensitivity. And you can't do that when you are not relaxed."

"I guess that's true."

After a few more minutes practice he added, "When do people learn the most?"

I thought about it for a second. "Probably when they are little kids."

"That's right. From birth to age five. We learn to walk, feed ourselves, talk, recognize people and things, go to the bathroom, ride a bike, maybe swim."

All the time I'm thinking, 'Yeah, and you probably mastered two or three martial arts by the time you were five.'

"Kids learn all this stuff, and they have fun doing it."

"So what's the right approach to training, then, Sifu?"

"It depends on the situation and the person. It has to be a balance. Like raising children."

I was anxious to hear this analogy.

"You can't be too loose and let them do whatever they want, because they need some guidance. But if you are too overbearing they will never experience things for themselves. Children grow up and go in all different directions. Like popcorn," he said as his fingers shot out all over the place.

"You can't predict where it will go. But if you keep it in the pot, then it's still good enough to eat. In the beginning, you have to provide guidance and some structure. Otherwise, they will get out and not know what to do. Like the popcorn. It will get stepped on and crushed. Learning is the same.

"In martial arts if you try to kill your partner on every shot, you won't understand the basics. It will be very difficult for you to acquire the sensitivity and timing you need to get really good. Not to mention, no one will want to work out with you.

"So when you train, go easy at first. Okay? Then, later, when you have the technique, you can speed up and the power will be there. But don't rush or you will lose your technique, and your power, and all of your friends."

That is not to say that Sifu Fong doesn't train himself or his students hard. There have been times when I could barely lift my arms up to wash my hair after a session with him. After virtually every training my forearms are black and blue from wrist to elbow. And during tests, he'll go hard. If you miss, you get hit, hard.

But when he teaches, it is slow, and encouraging. Testing is one thing, teaching is another.

"Now, understanding that is easy. You are in the field of training, anyway, so you know this, right?"

"In my job I do, though in my personal life I forget on occasion," I admitted.

He laughed. "But teach your body this. You must focus on relaxing. Like a whip. A whip by itself is nothing. You can coil it up and hit me all day with it. Go ahead. I'm not gonna care," he said. He stood in a star shape, his legs and arms outstretched.

"But if someone uses the relaxed length to put force into the end," he said as he backed up, "then I'm going to care."

He went and got a focus mitt. It's a leather glove, like a catcher's mitt in baseball, with two inches of hard padding designed to absorb a punch. He gave it to me to put on and hold in front of my chest.

"So in the beginning you have to be loose and relaxed. Otherwise you will telegraph your intentions and your punch will be slow." He demonstrated in slow motion what he was saying.

"Then, at the last second, you focus your energy using the entire force of your body. That's how you get the power. From the ground coming all the way up."

He exploded into the mitt from only a couple of inches away. I was knocked back five feet. My chest felt like I had been hit by a sledge hammer. Luckily, he was going easy.

"You see?" he asked.

"Yes, sir." I felt it, too.

"So right away, tense, relax, tense, relax. Wing Chun is good for teaching that relaxation and sensitivity.

He looked at the clock. The end of another lesson.

"Be like a kid. Don't worry so much and you'll learn it. Focus on one thing at a time. And relax, have fun. That's why I'm always telling stories and jokes. I want people to relax and enjoy themselves, and breathe. If you don't breathe, you aren't going to relax. Like in Tai Chi, you relax. Some people call Wing Chun combat Tai Chi. So work on relaxing. Then from that state of relaxation, you can learn better. Just like a kid."

If my heart can become pure and simple like that of a child,
I think there can be no greater happiness than this.

—*Kitaro Nishida*

LOOK IN THE MIRROR

"Not many people know this, but Bruce's reach was that of someone who is six feet two, even though he was only five eight. His arms were very long. His hands were down almost to his knees. That's why you'll never see a picture of Bruce with his hands to his sides. His arms are always crossed.

"Because of that, he could do things that were to me almost magical," Dan Inosanto said. He backed up about six feet. "He'd be this far away, and before I could even react he would poke me in the forehead. I used to get so mad," he laughed. "How the heck can he do that?" he said as he scratched his head.

"He could do that because he had extraordinary attributes. He was born with them. The same thing with Michael Jordan. He can do things that none of us can do. For instance, can anyone here slam dunk a basketball?"

No one in the group raised their hand.

"See?" he said. "So we would have to adapt the techniques that he uses in order for them to work for us because he has certain attributes that we don't have. Just like I had to adapt some of Bruce's techniques because they didn't work for someone my size.

"So when you practice, you need to test things out and see what works for you. You have to make it your own. That's the art of it. In the beginning do what the teacher tells you, but then you have to adjust for your own specific characteristics. Are you following me?"

I answered positively, as did the other students in the group.

"You know a lot of people ask me why I study so many different arts. There are a lot of reasons, but one of them is that different martial arts help me develop different aspects better than others. Just as some artists do their best work in oil, or in clay, or through a song. I'm not a very good singer," he kidded, "so I practice martial arts. For you, though, figure out which kind of practice will help you develop the most. You have to be honest with yourself, though."

Guro Dan laughed. "You know when I started studying Kali and learned about the destructions, I thought, "No way. They aren't going to be able to do that to my jab."

A destruction is where a defender literally smashes the attacker's fist or foot with their own elbows and knees. It takes incredible timing and accuracy, and is something that certain styles have developed to a high degree.

"But then it happens to you and you change your mind. So if you're set in your ways you won't have a chance to develop. You need to be open to other possibilities and open to feedback about places you can grow and develop."

Most of us like to operate from our own areas of comfort. I think that's a normal reaction. We want to stay in our comfort zone, surrounded by experiences that are familiar, secure in the fact that we can handle situations that arise. But the world is not just one range, or just one climate, and if we limit ourselves only to what is comfortable, we will miss out. Like someone who grew up in alps and visits a rainforest in woolens and down. We have to understand the ranges or environments where we are strong. Then also seek to understand and develop in those areas where our experience is less.

When we start to expand in this way, it is sure to sometimes be uncomfortable. But refusing to be vulnerable is a sure path to rigidity and stagnation. When you expand your comfort zone, remember to take your time. Listen to what your partners and friends are telling you. See yourself clearly with all your imperfections. Accept them and move on. When you do, you will be able to enjoy any situation, whether familiar or not. Then you will be able to enjoy all four seasons and have fun, regardless of the weather.

> We are what we repeatedly do.
> Excellence, then, is not an act,
> but a habit.
>
> —*Aristotle*

YOUR TRUE TEACHERS

One of the students dropped his guard hand while attacking. His partner hit him in the face with a focus mitt and the first student's face turned beet red, more from anger than the smack. Sifu Fong saw what happened and called everyone to the center of the training room.

"Okay, everybody, look here." He asked the pair to repeat the drill as they just had, this time in slow motion.

"See? You have to keep your hand up," he said, slapping the attacker's back.

"Nobody likes to get hit. I don't, either. I bleed just like you do," Francis Fong said. "But only in the movies do people not get hit. My advice is this: if you don't want to get hit, don't fight. Just walk away."

He turned around and began walking out of the room, provoking a chorus of chuckles from all of us. He came back to the center of the group.

"When someone hits you in practice, don't get mad. Instead, you better thank them. Somebody hits me, I say, 'Oh, thank you. You showed me what I was doing wrong.'" he laughed.

"They are your best teachers. Not the ones that sweet talk you and tell you how great you are. The people that point out your mistakes are the ones who help you the most. You better buy them a present."

If you don't want to get hit, don't fight.

—Francis Fong

THE SIXTH KEY

SHARE WITH OTHERS

When you look back on your life,
the times that will stand out will be
the ones where you did things for others.

—Anonymous

I remember one weekend afternoon when I was a young boy, my Dad asked me and my two brothers and two sisters if we wanted some candy. Of course we said yes. So he broke his candy bar into five pieces. Three of them were about the same size. Of the remaining two pieces, one was much bigger than any of the others, the other much smaller. He asked us to point to the piece that we wanted. Everyone else pointed to the biggest one. I said that I'd take the smallest one so the other kids could have more. Now I'm not saying that this is what I always did, but it was the way it happened that day. And, while all the other kids were hoping they would get the biggest piece, he gave it to me. Because I was willing to share and let others get more, he gave me more.

Isn't that a common sentiment? For those of you with kids, how do you feel when your child is selfish and won't share? Do you want to give him or her more? No way. It's like your actions mirror theirs. The more they clutch to things and are unwilling to share, the more you restrict your giving to them.

On the other hand, if your child shares freely and openly with others, you want to give them more. You want them to have more. You feel good when they succeed because their success helps others. Just like it feels good to give selflessly to someone else. You give with no thought of what you get in return, but because you want to help that person, or make their day a little brighter. It feels great, doesn't it? Or, how about when someone does something nice for you? Don't you feel like doing something for them in return, even if they didn't ask you? It's the Golden Rule: *Do Unto Others As You Would Have Them Do Unto You.*

We all learned this back when we were little kids. Well, we were all told this when we were little kids, anyway. But sometimes, in this hustle and bustle world of fast results and next quarter myopia, that can get lost. It's real easy to get caught up in doing our own thing, and not taking the time to share what we know with others. Indeed, we are often told not to share what we know with others in order not to lose our competitive edge.

One of the characteristics that separates a master from an expert, maybe more than any other, is that the master understands the cycle of learning. He or she knows that we all pass through different stages and levels as we learn new skills and behaviors. Some masters use the model of learning passed down by craftsmen of old: apprentice, journeyman, craftsman and master. They know that there are skills to be learned at each level, and that a good student never stops seeking out new knowledge.

A master knows that he or she got to where they are through the help of others. Their humility is not just a downplaying of their skills, but, rather, recognizing that regardless of your level of expertise, you can always expand yourself through contact with others.

A master shares freely of his or her skills because they know that with each person who grows from that contact, so will they, too, be enriched. Because of this understanding, they are willing to help others get even better than they themselves are. Masters want their students to surpass them. There's no point in hoarding your knowledge to yourself, it only makes everyone go hungry. Masters are committed to sharing their knowledge with others, and ask their students to do the same.

When Francis Fong accepted me as an apprentice instructor, he told me what he expected of me. After he was done outlining what I must do to remain a certified instructor, he added one more important thing.

"I'm not teaching you just for yourself. I'm sharing what I know, my experience, with you so that you can share it with other people."

This is the sixth key in the path of mastery.

COOPERATION VERSUS COMPETITION

"Sifu, what do you think is the most important thing in the martial arts?" I said.

"Respect is most important. It's not about who's better than who, or who is afraid of who. It's about helping each other, teaching each other. That's the only way you can get better. You have to help each other.

"You can't go like this." Francis Fong smashed his fists together, knuckle to knuckle. "That kind of competition is no good. It's better like this." He faced his hands together, palms almost touching, going up in tandem.

"Cooperate. Push each other to get better. That's the best way. Sometimes you will be better, so teach your partner. Sometimes others will be better than you, so hopefully they will share what they know with you."

"Yes, sir," I said. We continued training for another thirty or forty minutes before the next break. During that time I had another question.

"Sifu, you came to this country in 1973, right?"

He nodded.

"So, when you started your school, you must have had a lot of beginners studying with you."

"That's right," he said.

"So how did you get any better? I mean, you had to be so much better than anyone you trained with."

"You can learn from anyone, and you will see your mistakes in somebody else. You can only see your own mistakes. The ones you point out are really your own. So when you teach someone else, you learn a lot from them. I always learn from somebody else. It doesn't matter what skill level they are. That's why you should always work together with other people.

"There used to be all this secrecy in martial arts. No one shared anything with anyone else. That's no good. It's better to be open. Everyone has the same problems. Different languages, but we all say the same thing. Just help everyone you can, that way we all get better together."

You must become the change you seek in the world.
—*Mohandis "Mahatma" Ghandi*

THE CRAB

"I was studying Malaysian Bersilat with Mustafa and with John DeJong in Indonesian Pentjak Silat, and these guys were fighting like this, down in a crouch like a crab." Dan Inosanto dropped down into an almost seated position, just a few inches from the ground, and moved rapidly across the floor.

"It looks silly, doesn't it?" he said as he stood up. "You think you can just kick them in the head. That's what I thought, too. But if a guy drops down like this, you better run. Otherwise, you'll be dead in eight seconds."

I didn't know if he meant that literally or figuratively, though he seemed pretty serious, so I decided not to ask.

"See, they are used to fighting like that against someone who stands up, but we aren't used to fighting someone who is sitting. So train with all kinds of styles. That day I got it taken to me in unarmed combat, I'll have to admit. Though the next day I fared better with weapons," he grinned.

"But share what you know. That's the only way to learn. Don't stop and think that your way is the only way. I routinely train with and learn from instructors who are both younger than me, and less experienced in the eyes of the martial arts community. I can learn from and appreciate what they have to offer.

"Bruce would study all different styles—Wing Chun, Karate, Kung Fu, Jujitsu, Fencing, Grappling, Boxing—anything, and see what he liked. He took what was useful for him. The best way to improve is to share with others, constantly expose yourself to other ideas and approaches."

He walked over to his equipment bag and pulled out an eighteen inch machete.

"Now when you go to Southeast Asia, people carry these knives around with them. Not like here, where just criminals do, everyone. That's just what they do."

Guro Dan took an on-guard position.

"So this changes your outlook. What are you going to say, I have an awesome side kick? They'll cut your foot off! So when you share with other people you learn what works in different situations. You learn, and so do they. Otherwise, you never grow."

Of course, the flip side means being able to accept instruction from anyone, even an eight year old kid! The other day, I was working out with some of my training partners. As I often do on weekends, I had brought my son Danny with me. Danny has always loved training and is living up to his name by being quite an accomplished martial artist. On this day he and I were working on some Sumbrada patterns. It's an exercise for practicing stick coordination, and each partner takes turns attacking and defending, practicing set moves.

After Danny and I had been practicing for a while, I had to go off to take a phone call. I came back to see my little son working out with my six foot three training partner Jerry who weighs over two hundred and fifty pounds. And there was Danny, barely tall enough to reach Jerry's waist teaching him the Sumbrada pattern. And, to his credit, Jerry was open to this slightly unorthodox arrangement and learning the moves.

Lots of martial arts instructors are afraid to do what Dan Inosanto was describing. They are afraid that by sharing what they know, they will be weaker than their student. They don't want to give away their secrets. Lots of us walk around feeling like, "I'm stronger than you because I know something you don't." We think we have to protect ourselves by keeping others in the dark. But that is a surefire path to declining our strength as a people, a family or an organization. The only way we can grow is to take Guro Dan's advice, open ourselves to those around us so we can all learn. And if our students or children or even employees surpass us, well, that's great. It means that we as a family, or nation are growing stronger. It also gives us incentive to grow along with them.

A university student went to visit a Zen master. The master soon realized that instead of coming to learn, the student was trying to impress him with his knowledge of Zen. The master suggested they have tea, and began by filling the student's cup. When it was full, he kept on pouring. The master continued, and tea went all over the table and onto the floor. The student couldn't hold back any longer.

"It's full already. You can't fit any more in!" he exclaimed. The Zen master stopped pouring and smiled.

"You are like this cup. You are so full of your own notions that you are unable to take in anything new." With that, the master picked up the student's cup and turned it over, emptying the tea.

"To learn, you must first empty your cup."

—*Zen Story*

THE STRONGEST MUSCLE

"What do you think your strongest muscle is?" Gurucharan asked me one day while we were driving around Boston.

I thought for a moment. "Either the muscles in your back or legs, I would guess. But those are groups of muscles. I don't know. I guess the legs."

He shook his head. "The tongue."

I pushed my tongue against the roof of my mouth. It seemed a little strong, but not that much.

"One word from your tongue can cut down a person immediately, it can destroy them. Or it can lift them up. Don't speak carelessly. Understand the power of the word. Lift people up, encourage them, be a source of light and inspiration."

As we drove around the city, I thought about how ever since my kids were little, I would tell them "secrets" at night. I would whisper in their ears how much I loved them, and that I was proud of them, then I would tell them something I really liked that they had done that day, or what I admired about them in general. It was a small ritual I did to help them sleep, and let them know I was there for them.

As they got older, I thought they would grow out of it. As they entered the more realistic minded years of pre-adolescence, I expected them to think of it as stupid or babyish. But, now, if I forget to do it, they always come up to me, turn their heads, and say, "secrets."

Sharing with others isn't just knowledge, it's also support, encouragement and love.

The love you fail to share is the only pain you'll ever live with.
—*Brian Biro*

THE SEVENTH KEY

SURRENDER

Can you walk on water?
You have done no better than a straw.
Can you fly in the air?
You have done no better than a bluebottle.
Conquer your heart;
then you may become somebody.

—*Ansari of Herat*

We had decided to turn our attic into a master bedroom, and so, for about six months, I would work on it every evening for a few hours after dinner. One night, when David was about four, he came up and asked how it was going. Like usual, I didn't look at him when he asked the question. I was busy painting. I kept up my work and, without much attention, said that it was okay, but that it was a little lonely.

"I'll bet it is," he said in a voice so full of compassion that it brought tears to my eyes. I set down my roller, looked him in his beautiful blue eyes, and hugged him to me. The tears did fall as I felt his little arms wrap around my waist.

The compassion and seriousness with which he answered my off-hand comment opened a flood-gate of emotion in me. Here was my four year old son teaching me about lessons I was still struggling to grasp. I was missing so much with my single minded determination to finish the task before me. I could have taken five minutes to spend with him, given him a hug and sent him back downstairs. But here I was again, eating without tasting, missing the flavor of the food. Rushing to finish the job and ignoring this small person who is so important to me.

For me, surrender in part means understanding that things take time. That time and the natural pace of things is what we fight against so much in our busy world and efforts to get things done. For so many years I had this idea that I had to control everything—my businesses, my emotions, my children. I was so driven to succeed that I lost track of what I was succeeding for.

A farmer, harvesting his crop, would never try to pull the wheat to make it grow faster, or yell at the orange to hurry up and ripen. People close to nature understand there is a natural rhythm to life and you will be happiest if you can align yourself with it. That means understanding the results you want and surrendering to your own capabilities.

Remember, you already have the ability in yourself to accomplish more than you ever thought. Let go of things that hold you back. Instead of accumulating, simplify.

I don't really have a single story or lesson to relate that will explain exactly how to accomplish this concept of surrendering. There isn't just one event that transformed my life; rather, over time, things changed till I look back now and see the path.

Because I wanted to be the kind of person who can evince those characteristics I saw in my teachers, wanted it with all my heart, I found my everyday behaviors start to change. I wasn't working towards a specific goal, but a way of being every day.

By studying with these masters, I have learned many, many valuable lessons. But of all of them, this one was the most important.

There's a poem that says:

God, grant me the serenity
to accept the things I cannot change,
the courage to change the things I can,
and the wisdom to know the difference.

Though each of these teachers teach through different means, they all are going to the same destination. They understand that we have the potential to be incredibly powerful people, and also realize that true power comes from the heart.

Surrender to me means unclenching your heart. Not always having to be right, but knowing that you have tried your best. It comes back to the first key. The masters have taught me that surrender is trying your best, acknowledging that, and stepping back with the trust and faith that things will work out as they are supposed to.

TRYING TOO HARD

"Sifu, in your experience, what prevents people from improving in Wing Chun the most?" We were wrapping up a private training session down at his academy in Atlanta, and he asked me if I had any questions.

Francis Fong answered immediately. "Trying too hard."

That surprised me. "Really? I would have thought that they don't try hard enough."

"There's some of that, too. But more often people try too hard. They want to get the result right away. They want to achieve the result instead of being the kind of person who could get that result."

I knew I was guilty of that. When I started Wing Chun, I had already earned a second degree black belt in Tae Kwon Do, a purple belt in Isshin Ryu Karate, had trained in a number of other styles, and had wrestled competitively in both high school and college, so I was used to doing well and used to progressing quickly. I figured that since I had done well in other things, I could expect the same results with Wing Chun, too.

"Wing Chun takes a lot of patience and time. It's not for everyone. People want to walk away dripping with sweat every time. They want a good workout. If that's all people want, that's easy. No problem. I can give it to them."

I was one of those people. Even though I enjoyed my Wing Chun training, there were times when I felt that I hadn't worked out enough. Sometimes I would barely even break a sweat. That bothered me because I felt like I wasn't working out hard enough. I told Sifu Fong about that.

"First train your mind. If you develop your mind, then your body will come along. So when you train your mind, why should you sweat?" He laughed.

"You know people say, 'No sweat'? Why? Because

it's easy, they don't worry. The same thing. If you sweat just thinking, then there's something wrong with you."

I couldn't help laughing.

"So just train your mind first." He gestured for me to continue the drill that we had begun the session with, one that at first I was having a lot of difficulty with.

"Ah, see? Now you've got it. You are relaxed. Your mind knows what to do, so your body doesn't have to work so hard," he said.

"No sweat."

"Right, no sweat. Now in some things you need to sweat, like to condition your body. If you run or lift weights, or do sparring rounds, then of course you will sweat. It depends on the activity. But just to do the physical activity without developing your mind is no good."

"Yes, sir," I answered. We continued the drill for a few more minutes, then he suggested we take a break.

"I think that's why a lot of people get so tired when they begin training," I said. "They usually think it's because they are in poor shape, but really I think it's more because they don't relax."

Sifu Fong nodded. "That's it. You can run, jump rope, hit the heavy bag, whatever you want. But if your mind is not relaxed, it won't matter. After thirty seconds you'll be gasping for air, looking for your oxygen mask."

"And your body will never relax if your mind doesn't first, right Sifu?"

"Yes, that's why I say work on your mind first. The body will follow," he said.

"Sometimes it's hard for me to slow down like that, just train my mind. I want to learn it quickly and get the workout."

"Use your mind, train and develop it, it's the most powerful tool you have. Besides, what's your rush?" he said.

I couldn't give him an immediate answer.

"Is it the moves you want to learn?"

"Yes, Sifu, I do."

"But why? You already know a lot of moves, don't you?"

I admitted that I did, not like him, though.

"Don't compare yourself to me. You have already gotten a black belt, so you know a lot of moves, but knowing the moves hasn't given you what you wanted, has it?"

Once again he was right.

"Remember. Master yourself. It doesn't matter if you can kick the sky if you aren't happy with yourself."

I nodded my head. "I guess I just want to advance quickly."

"The desire is good, just remember that before you can learn, you must let your mind relax. Taking your time and slowing down so that you learn properly is much harder. It's easy to work out hard and keep doing the same thing over and over, but that isn't how we grow. Keep doing that and you will never progress, and not just in martial arts."

I smiled, though I was lost in thought. I wondered why I pushed myself so hard for the results. What was I looking for? "I guess I just want to do well, that's why I push so hard," I told him.

He nodded as if to say that there was something more.

"Well, actually, I probably did it out of fear."

Sifu Fong smiled. He seemed to like that answer better.

I didn't seem like someone acting from fear, though. I had been full contact fighting for years. I had started three businesses on my own, businesses in which I had absolutely no experience. I remember when I bought my first one, a fish market and seafood restaurant, I didn't even know the names of any of the fish, except for cod. I didn't know how to cook fish, cut it, clean it. I almost threw up the first day from the smell alone.

But I jumped into it with both feet. As I told him that story, I thought about how I had started training in boxing. Because I had had experience in what could be called combative arts for over fifteen years, I figured I would be good at it right away.

My partner and I sparred full out on the very first day. I got hit so much I couldn't see a thing besides his big red gloves. The only thing I proved that day was that I could take a punch. Something, actually, that I proved over and over that day.

So why didn't I go slow and relax? Sifu Fong's comment about always wanting to work out hard described me exactly. If I couldn't wring out my T-shirt after a class, I viewed it as time wasted.

But that belief system prevented me from learning anything new. I wouldn't allow myself to slow down enough to learn it, I had to do it fast and strong, so I would feel fast and strong, instead of slow. I had put so much pressure on myself to succeed, that would only do the same thing over and over again, instead of relaxing and trusting that the results would come.

I was getting really proficient in a narrow band of skills.

I didn't want to be a beginner, again. Somewhere I got it stuck in my head that if I wasn't perfect, strong and invincible, then I was no good. I was afraid of failing, of not being good enough, of not having the answers. Unfortunately that fear was not isolated to my martial arts practice alone. It was only magnified there.

"So take your time. Don't rush. Go slow. When you practice, don't worry about hitting. Concentrate on your position. Don't worry if it takes you a long time. The longer it takes you to learn it, the longer it will stay with you.

"In your life there will be situations that are new to you, that you won't have experience dealing with. Don't worry, go slow. Focus on what you can do. Ask for help, watch other people. Don't stiffen up and think you have to know everything. The only way you get better is practice, and when you do you are going to make a lot of mistakes. That's the only way to improve. But you have to give yourself permission to make mistakes."

Sifu Fong looked at the clock. Our one hour private session had gone over by thirty-five minutes. It was time for me to get to the Atlanta airport, anyway.

"Okay, Jim, see you later," he said as we hugged goodbye.

My mind flashed to another hug, many years earlier.

My mother was the ultimate stay at home mom. She would be there every day when we came home, always attending our after school activities, and delighted with the accomplishments of all five of her children. During the summers growing up we would stay up late almost every night playing Scrabble, laughing at our awful jokes, talking and then going out to Dee's Donuts around midnight. She was a great mom.

When I was a freshman in college she was diagnosed with breast cancer. She seemed okay on the phone when she called to tell me, but admitted that she was a little scared. I was scared, too, but I couldn't tell her.

When I came home for Christmas break she had lost all her hair because of the chemotherapy. She had also gained a lot of weight, something she struggled with under normal conditions. I wanted to hug her and cry and tell her that I was scared, but I couldn't. I didn't know how.

Over the next seven years she had times that she did very well, and some setbacks. For a while, though, it seemed as if she had made a full recovery. The doctors said she was in remission, but it turned out that she wasn't, and her cancer came back. It had spread to her spine. It had infused itself into and between her vertebrae. At first the tumors pressing against her spinal cord resulted in a tingling sensation in her feet and legs. Within a month it resulted in her being paralyzed from the waist down.

The tumors in the rest of her spine didn't cause paralysis, but rather, excruciating pain. Often times I would hear her cry out in the middle of the night the pain got so bad.

She would always ask me to sit with her and talk. I would, for a few minutes, but invariably I would excuse myself. I had a brand new business to run, one that I had a hundred and fifty grand riding on, and one that needed constant attention. I also had a young wife and two infants to take care of at the time, so our visits were never long, I had too many other important things to attend to. I didn't want to admit to her or myself that witnessing her in such debilitating pain left me with feelings of helplessness I didn't know what to do with.

After a while the morphine pills didn't even touch her pain, and the doctor switched her to an intravenous pump. Though the higher dosages worked to ease her pain, it took its toll in other ways. Soon her pleasant, easy-going personality was replaced by a demanding, desperate one. Being with her was not the same.

The night I received the call that she was on her death bed is probably the most vivid memory I carry with me to this day. It was a Friday evening, about five-thirty, the busiest hour of the seventy-two that we were open in a week. It was my brother Brian.

"Tell him I'll call him back. We're getting slammed."

My wife, Jessie, motioned for me to come to the back office. "He's at the hospital. You better take it."

My legs turned to concrete as I willed myself towards the phone. My usual commanding voice was replaced by a weak hello. My brother told me the doctors said she wouldn't make it through the night. Her liver and kidneys had shut down, and that I better come right away.

I slumped to the floor. The legs that had carried me on thousands of miles of runs and that had lifted tons of weight could no longer support me. Jessie helped me up. She urged me to go right away, saying she would soon follow.

All of us were around her hospital bed watching her. She fought to draw every breath. We watched in horror as her heart rate climbed to over a hundred and fifty beats per minute, then gradually and sickeningly slowed to nothing.

I hugged her after she passed away. I couldn't recall the last time I had held her. I don't know if I cried more because she had died or because of what I hadn't done when she was alive.

I had been working out since I was twelve to build up my body so I would be strong and confident. And I did that. I was very strong, and confident.

But I also discovered that the same walls that protected me also held me prisoner. I wasn't allowing for feelings of not knowing what to do, of not being perfect. I didn't realize that compassion, vulnerability and not knowing are also very powerful.

Sifu Fong had no way of knowing how much that lesson meant to me. Somehow I hoped that my Mom would.

The soft overcomes the hard;
the gentle overcomes the rigid.
Everyone knows this is true,
but few can put it into practice.

—*Lao-tzu, Tao te ching*

LET GOD TAKE OVER

"One time we were doing a particularly difficult exercise, and Yogi Bhajan left the room. As he was leaving he said, 'Keep going, I'll be right back', and goes into the men's room," Gurucharan said.

"The same Yogi Bhajan who was left in the tree for three days? Did that give you a lot of confidence that his definition of right back was the same as yours?" I asked.

Gurucharan laughed. "Not really. Anyway, we were all doing this rather difficult exercise, and we were getting pretty tired, sweat was pouring down our faces, and our arms were dropping lower and lower, and after five or six minutes we were all kind of wondering what was going on. Then we heard the toilet flush.

"So we all got this renewed energy, and we started breathing more strongly and our arms were back up, and two more minutes went by. No Yogi Bhajan. Another minute went by, still no Yogi Bhajan. And we're thinking, 'What's he doing? Re-tying his turban?'

"Finally, he comes out. 'Oh, are you still going?' he says. 'I was only going to have you do three minutes. But since you did eleven minutes on that side, you have to balance it out and do eleven minutes on the other side.'

"We all just about fainted right then and there. But see, a master will give you exercises that are impossible to do without surrendering. They get you to see that there is a limit to the finite self, the you and your strength, so you see that the strength of the infinite is unlimited. So just when you think 'I can't go on!,' they teach: 'You don't have to. You did your part. You showed up. Let God take over. Have faith.'

"So you surrender. You do what you can as a human being, with all your strengths and determination and talent and your weaknesses, then you step back—and let God take over. So you give your arms to God, let him hold them up. You give your problems to God, let him deal with them. You do your part, then there is a time for surrender.

"That," Gurucharan said, "is mastery."

> Even if our efforts of attention seem for
> years to be producing no result,
> one day a light that is in exact proportion
> to them will flood the soul.
>
> —*Simone Weil*

FAITH

I had just been informed that I would be moving to another position as a result of a consolidation of certain groups. That meant that Jeff McLeod would no longer be my manager. As excited as I was about the potential the new position had, I felt a sense of loss at not having the day to day interaction with Jeff that I had enjoyed for over a year.

I had learned such a tremendous amount from him, and I invited him to breakfast to tell him that.

"Jeff, one more thing I'd like to ask you, if you don't mind."

He nodded to indicate I should continue.

"You have taught me so much over this past year, both by what you have said and by who you are. Your character."

Jeff shook his head. He is not one for receiving compliments.

"A lot of people have told me things that are similar to what you have said. But doing it—acting that way in the midst of pressures—that is another matter entirely. What do you do or believe that allows you to act that way?" I said.

Jeff paused. "Do you really want to know?"

I smiled in response.

"Jim, I can't answer that question without talking about God."

"Please do," I prompted.

"I do the best I can, and leave the rest up to God. When I pray, I share my problems with him. Think about it. As a father, you would do anything to help your child, wouldn't you?"

"Absolutely."

"But you would have to know about it. If you don't know, you can't help them. Haven't you had that experience where you find out about something your kid did after the fact? And then it's too late to help?"

I agreed that I had.

"When I pray, I tell God everything. He is all knowing, all powerful. I do my best, and step back."

Love God and do what you will.

—*St. Augustine*

BREAK THE MOLD

"Bruce Lee used to say, 'Make the mold, then break the mold.' What he meant was that you need a mold, some kind of structure, to learn. Just like when you begin playing the piano, you don't play your own music. You learn scales, then you play other people's pieces," Dan Inosanto said.

"But at the highest level, you transcend all that. You go beyond what other people have done to create your own music. Like a jazz musician.

"That's what mastering something is all about. It's trusting what you know, and surrendering to what you don't know so that your unconscious can take over."

If you have to ask,
you'll never know what jazz is.

—Louis Armstrong

"It's like a hose. If you kink it up then grab on to it, the pressure of the water will push up against the sides. So to grab on it feels strong. But actually, that is not power, that is tension," Francis Fong said.

"So relax to get the power?" I said.

"The power only comes when you release the binds and blocks, in this case the kink, and let the water flow freely. Containing is not power, holding on is not power.

"Flowing is power, flowing is energy, flowing is life. When you feel the hose as the water rushes out, that is power. It's almost electric. Not totally slack so that you're a blob, and not so tense that you can't move, but in between. A balance. Just relax. Your natural muscle tone is enough."

Sifu Fong sat down on a nearby chair.

"You know, Jim, a lot of people want to be so tough. I say, 'You think you're tough? There's always someone tougher than you. You think you're strong? Always someone stronger. You think you're crazy? Go to a mental hospital. There are a lot of people crazier than you.'"

I laughed along with him.

"That way is not the answer. It will never be enough to fill your emptiness. The more you run after it, the more you will need. That way is a trap. It will never be enough because you will never be enough. Understand what I'm saying?"

I had lived it for too many years. My simple answer belied the depth of my understanding. "Yes, Sifu, I do."

Though Francis Fong is usually very talkative, he was silent for quite a while before he spoke again.

"The real power comes from love. God is love. Some people go to church to feel God, some people go to a temple. Some people sing to feel God. Some people paint to feel God. Some people practice martial arts to feel God."

Each and every master, regardless of the era or place,
heard the call and attained harmony with heaven and earth.
There are many paths leading to the top of Mount Fuji,
but only one summit - love.

—Morihei Ueshiba, founder of Aikido

THE SEVEN KEYS

THE SEVEN KEYS

I chose the term keys very deliberately. I could have said the seven principles, laws or concepts, but they don't convey the same meaning as a key.

A key can unlock something that you want. The thing is, though, you need it every time. You don't unlock your house, then throw away your key. "Well, glad that's done."

Not at all. You need that key every time you want to get to where you want to be.

These seven keys are just the same. If you are dedicated and put forth a lot of effort, you could probably get pretty good results without these keys. But in my experience of working with thousands of people in seminars, workshops, and private training, I haven't seen people attain long lasting success without them. Even those who do get excellent results generally don't possess the inner peace that comes from using the lessons described within these pages.

I said at the beginning of this book that the path of mastery is an approach to life, not a destination. Therefore, my wish is that the teachings of these masters and the insights that I have shared with you has in some way helped you on your journey. I encourage you to share these keys with others, and I thank you for sharing your time with me and my teachers.

Oh, one last thing. Always remember to bring your keys.

GLOSSARY OF THE MASTERS

photograph by John Barfield

Francis Fong is considered by many to be one of the finest Wing Chun instructors in the United States. Sifu Francis Fong began his study in the art of Wing Chun Kung Fu under Sifu Jiu Wan in Hong Kong in 1965. He decided to come to the United States, arriving in New York in 1973, and eventually settling in Atlanta, GA, in 1975, where he opened the Francis Fong Academy.

Sifu Fong has trained police special officers and S.W.A.T. teams, as well as the Fort Benning Rangers, in close quarters tactics. He is currently working with the U.S. government on an updated Army training manual regarding Wing Chun, Kali and Muay Thai principles. He is a full instructor in Kali under Dan Inosanto and is also the Southeastern representative for the Thai Boxing Association USA under the direction of Master "Chai" Sirisute.

Sifu Fong was nominated for instructor of the year in *Inside Kung Fu* magazine in 1988 and appeared on the cover in January 1988. In addition to his astonishing abilities and dedication to Wing Chun, as an instructor Sifu Fong is highly communicative, demonstrating and teaching with incredible energy, skill, and tireless enthusiasm.

To find out about his classes in Atlanta, or the location of his nationwide seminars, call the Francis Fong Martial Arts Academy at (770) 623-8090.

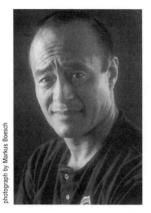

Dan Inosanto is the man personally chosen by Bruce Lee to carry on the concepts and philosophy of Jeet Kune Do. His remarkable ability, communicative skills and warm personality have prompted martial artists the world over to travel to meet him. In addition to having studied over twenty methods of Filipino Martial Arts, he has studied with such experts as Ed Parker, Bruce Lee, Chai Sirisute, John LaCoste, Ben Largusa, Paul deThouars, Herman Suwanda, Yori Nakamura and many others.

To find our more about the Insanto Academy in Los Angeles, California, his nationwide seminars, or books, videos and other products, call (310) 348-9944.

Jeff McLeod is a native of Dothan, Alabama, which is still his favorite place. After graduating from Morehouse College, he began his career with Eastman Kodak Company where he is currently General Manager and Vice President of Kodak Professional for the United States and Canada.

Jeff and his wife Gloria have two sons, Jeremy and Jeffrey. In addition to time with his family, Jeff enjoys working with young men in his local church as a sponsor of their developmental activities and as a mentor. He also serves as a member on the board of directors for several organizations.

He attributes any positive impact he has on others to the inner strength that he derives from his belief in God; the strong influence of his parents (who modeled what it really means to put others first and do what is right); and the exceptional mentors and very special people who are unsung heroes in his life.

Gurucharan Singh Khalsa, Ph.D., is an expert in Kundalini Yoga as taught by Yogi Bhajan, Ph.D., and has been Yogi Bhajan's student and a compiler of his teachings since 1969. Dr. Khalsa combines Western scientific training with Eastern traditions to develop practical approaches to personal growth and organizational success. He has a keen understanding of Humanology, the psychology of personal excellence developed by Yogi Bhajan, and has used it in clinical practice for over 20 years.

Dr. Khalsa is president of Khalsa Consultants, Inc. in Wellesley, MA. The company provides seminars, products and personal coaching to develop individual's talents, and maintain high performance in business. He is currently an instructor of yoga and wellness psychology at the Massachusetts Institute of Technology.

Dr. Khalsa is also a co-founder of the Kundalini Research Institute and has led teacher trainings for KRI and 3HO since 1971. He is committed to progress in both spiritual and social arenas. He is a Mukhia Singh Sahib, a minister, in Sikh Dharma and an active member of the Khalsa Council that serves all of Sikh Dharma. He has worked in and designed programs for rehabilitation from drug use, for prison populations, and for youth education.

For information on classes in the Boston area, nationwide seminars and products, call (617) 237-7305.

About the Author

Jim Brault has spent nearly two decades searching out and sharing with others what he terms the Path of Mastery—keys to obtaining peak performance and the inner peace, allowing you to enjoy your results with the ones you care most about. His journey has led him to study with some of the most gifted teachers of our time.

Jim began his study of martial arts in 1983. After earning a second degree black belt in Tae Kwon Do, he went on to study several different arts. He earned his Apprentice Instructor Certification in Wing Chun Kung Fu under Sifu Francis Fong in 1996. He is also a certified instructor of Kundalini Yoga and meditation.

Jim earned his B.A. in Psychology from the State University of New York at Binghamton, and his M.A. from Cornell University in Industrial and Labor Relations. He currently is the Director of Sales and Customer Training for Eastman Kodak Company.

Jim teaches Wing Chun classes twice weekly, and lives with his wife, Jessie, and three children, Rachel, David and Danny in Rochester, NY.